MONTH-BY-MONTH

PHONICS

FOR THIRD GRADE

SYSTEMATIC, MULTILEVEL INSTRUCTION

by
Patricia M. Cunningham
and
Dorothy P. Hall

DEDICATION

This book is dedicated to third grade teachers everywhere who take fledgling readers and writers and turn them into independent learners.

TABLE OF CONTENTS

INTRODUCTION

Phonics is the current "hot topic." Everyone is talking about phonics and everyone has an opinion about what should be taught, and how and when it should be taught. **Phonics *is* an important part of reading instruction, but phonics is not all that matters.** In fact, children who come to school with limited reading experiences and who are taught in a "phonics first, phonics only" approach often get the idea that reading is "sounding out words!" You do have to figure out words, but reading is not figuring out words and "sounding good." Figuring out words is the means to the end of understanding, learning, thinking, and enjoying reading. Good readers do use phonics to figure out some words, but good readers also recognize the most-frequent words instantly as sight words. They use context to check that what they are reading and the words they have figured out make sense.

The word *balance* is currently in danger of extinction from overuse, but the concept of balance is and will remain a critically-important idea. To us, balance in reading instruction is like a balanced diet. We eat from the different food groups because each group of foods is important to growth. We decide how much of each group should be included in a balanced diet, and these amounts change as people grow older. We do not try to decide which of the different groups is best, nor do we go through phases in which "experts" recommend that we eat only from one group!

To become good readers, students need a balanced reading diet. The different "food groups" of balanced reading instruction are Guided Reading, Self-Selected Reading, Writing, and Working with Words. See *The Teacher's Guide to the Four Blocks®* by Cunningham, Hall, and Sigmon (Carson-Dellosa, 1999); *The Administrator's Guide to the Four Blocks®* by Hall and Cunningham (Carson-Dellosa, 2003); *Guided Reading the Four-Blocks® Way* by Cunningham, Hall, and Cunningham (Carson-Dellosa, 2000); *Self-Selected Reading the Four-Blocks® Way* by Cunningham, Hall, and Gambrell (Carson-Dellosa, 2002); *Classrooms That Work: They Can All Read and Write* (3rd ed.) by Cunningham and Allington (Allyn and Bacon, 2003); *The Four-Blocks® Literacy Model: How and Why It Really Works* video with Pat Cunningham (Carson-Dellosa, 2001); and *Month-by-Month Phonics for Third Grade* video with Pat Cunningham (Carson-Dellosa, 2002) for detailed descriptions of all Four Blocks.

This book provides month-by-month activities for one-quarter of a well-balanced reading diet—the Working With Words block. When this block is combined with the other essential components—Guided Reading, Self-Selected Reading, and Writing—readers grow and enhance their literacy skills at their optimum rates.

The Four-Blocks Approach to Phonics

As you begin this book, think about the kind of phonics instruction you will find here. **English is not a simple language to learn to decode and spell.** Many of the consonants and all of the vowels have a variety of sounds, depending on the surrounding letters. Vowels do not have just short and long sounds. This can be clearly understood by looking at any sentence and thinking about what the vowels do in that sentence. In the previous sentence, for example, these words contain the vowel **o**:

understood	looking	about	vowels	do

None of these **o**'s represent the short or long sound of **o**.

In the same sentence, these words contain the vowel **e**:

be	clearly	understood	sentence	vowels

The **e** in the word **be** represents the long **e** sound, and two of the three **e**'s in **sentence** represent the short sound of **e**. The **e** represents different sounds, not short or long, in **clearly**, **understood**, and **vowels**.

There is logic to the sounds represented by letters, including vowels, in English, but the logic is in the pattern—not in simple "vowel rules." Looking again at the words containing an **o**, we see that the two **o**'s in **understood** and **looking** have the same sound. We know that other **ood** and **ook** words, including **good**, **hood**, **cook**, and **shook**, share this same sound. The **ou** in **about** has the same sound that it has in other **out** words, including **out**, **shout**, and **clout**. The **ow** in **vowels** has the same sound in words such as **now**, **how**, and **cow**. Only the **o** in **do** does not follow a predictable pattern. If we look at the patterns in **clearly**, **understood**, and **vowels**, we see the **ear** representing the same sound as it does in **ear**, **hear**, and **dear**; the **er** representing the same sound it does in **her**, **mother**, and **father**; and the **-el** representing the same sound we hear in **towel**, **camel**, and **level**.

Phonics—the relationships between letters and sounds—makes sense in English, but only if you know to look for patterns of letters rather than individual letters. These patterns determine the sounds for consonant letters as well as vowels. **Psychologists tell us that the brain is a "pattern detector" and that separate, short, unknown words are separated by the brain into two patterns. These patterns are onsets (all of the letters up to the vowel) and rimes (the vowel and letters following it).** The first time we ever saw the words **spew**, **mite**, and **phrase**, we separated their onsets—**sp**, **m**, and **phr**—from their rimes—**ew**, **ite**, and **ase**—and then used what we knew about consonant and vowel patterns to come up with sounds for each part and combine them. **To be good decoders and spellers, children need to learn to quickly separate words into these parts, think of sounds associated with the patterns, and recombine them.** Because of the nature of English and the fact that the brain is a pattern detector, **the most useful approach to phonics instruction is one that teaches student to look for patterns from words they know and then use these patterns to read and spell unknown words.**

By the time students are in third grade, they are expected to be able to decode and spell most high-frequency words and short words that follow the patterns. Unfortunately, not all students meet this expectation. **The inability to decode and spell hinders them in all of their subjects and, until they become fluent with words, they make little progress and even fall further behind.** Even third graders who know high-frequency words and can decode and spell short words often **have difficulty with longer words.** The typical third-grade class contains a wide range of readers and writers, with many and varied decoding and spelling needs. This book contains a variety of multilevel activities which should help the range of third graders become fluent decoders and spellers.

The activities in this book are designed to meet five critical word fluency goals:

Goal 1	Teach students the correct spelling for high-frequency, often irregularly spelled words such as **they, friend, could, there, their, they're, right,** and **write**. *Word Wall*
Goal 2	Teach students how to decode and spell one- and two-syllable words based on patterns from words they already know. Students who can read **van, car,** and **jeep** should be able to decode and spell other rhyming words such as **plan, char,** and **steep**. *Using Words You Know, Making Words, Word Sorts and Hunts, Reading/Writing Rhymes*
Goal 3	Teach students that spelling rhyming words is not as easy as decoding them because some rhymes, such as **right/bite, claim/name,** and **toad/code**, have two spelling patterns. The reader has to develop a visual checking system and learn to use a dictionary when he is unsure about which pattern looks right. *Word Sorts and Hunts, Reading/Writing Rhymes, What Looks Right?*
Goal 4	Teach students that many "big" words are just smaller words combined as compounds or with endings, prefixes, and suffixes. Many polysyllabic words can be decoded and spelled if students look for meaningful "chunks" they know. *Word Wall* (words with prefixes and suffixes), *Making Words, Using Words You Know, Word Sorts and Hunts*
Goal 5	Teach students to use cross checking while reading and a visual checking system while writing to apply what they are learning as they engage in meaningful reading and writing. *Guess the Covered Word, What Looks Right?, Applying Strategies while Reading and Writing*

Each month's activities will include a variety of ways to help students meet these goals. As activities are introduced, their purpose and the type of students they will help most will be described. **Looking at the activities and your students, you should choose the activities which seem most appropriate.** You may also want to do some activities earlier or later in the year than suggested, based on the characteristics of your particular class.

Spelling in a Four-Blocks Classroom

The activities contained in *Month-by-Month Phonics for Third Grade* **cover the range of decoding and spelling skills important for most third-grade classes. Most teachers don't find it necessary to do an additional spelling program.** If, however, you need to use a spelling program, consider how you could do your spelling program "the Four-Blocks way." Most spelling programs are not very multilevel. The above average children can already spell the words and don't get much learning back for the time they spend on spelling. Struggling students may or may not learn the words for the test (depending on how much their parents drill them!) but they often can't spell these same words a month later and don't spell them correctly when writing. The activities here contain challenges for advanced third-grade spellers and different kinds of practice for children who need more than a week's worth of practice to learn words. The activities all emphasize "transfer" to similar words and to reading and writing.

Spelling programs are not very multilevel, and students often don't transfer what they learn to their writing. If you need to use a spelling program, try adapting the goals of your program with the activities in this book. If you must assign spelling exercises, assign them for homework. Parents feel that they know how to help with spelling, and you won't waste valuable class time with exercises which don't benefit the class.

We have had fun coming up with word activities that are active and challenging and have a sense of "puzzle solving" about them. We hope you and your students will enjoy working with words in some new ways and conclude that words are not only useful, but also fascinating!

Month at a Glance

A new school year, a new class of students, and some new ways to think about and work with words! A fresh start for you and the children! As you start the year, try to communicate an attitude of, "You're big kids now!" to your children. Children want to be older, more mature, and more grown-up, and third grade is the age at which they can begin to act in more mature, responsible ways—if they are expected to do so.

This month, use these three word activities with students:

- introducing *Word Wall*
- introducing *Using Words You Know*
- introducing *Guess the Covered Word*

Each activity is designed to set a tone of responsibility and maturity which, if you can communicate it to your students, will result in their becoming more independent in dealing with words as they read and write.

This book is written with the assumption that your third-grade classroom has the following characteristics:

- A lot of reading and writing are occurring—not just during language arts time, but during science, social studies, health, and math.

- Students are reading and discussing selections together, with partners or small groups.

- Students, when they need help with a word, are coaching each other to figure it out rather than just telling each other the word.

- Students are choosing pieces from first-draft writing and taking these pieces from "sloppy copy" to "(almost) published perfection."

- Students are helping each other revise and edit, and using dictionaries to resolve spellings they can't determine on their own.

- Students are making the transition from learning to read and write to reading and writing to learn.

It is likely that **your students are at all different levels in their reading and writing abilities:**

- **Some read and write quite well.** Even some of the best third-grade readers and writers, however, misspell some of the most frequent and irregular words, such as **they, friend,** and **where**.

- **Many students are good readers and can spell many words.** They may, however, still be using a letter-by-letter strategy for decoding and spelling rather than a more sophisticated pattern strategy.

- **Many third graders "know" more than they "use."** They can figure out a word when reading, or figure out how to spell a word when writing, if you are sitting with them. When reading and writing on their own, though, they don't use appropriate strategies. Psychologists call this "knowing when and where to do something" **metacognitive knowledge,** and third graders are at the perfect age to consolidate these metacognitive strategies.

- **Many third graders are still at beginning levels in reading and writing.** This does not mean they can't make rapid progress—it just means they haven't so far! When they reach third grade, many struggling readers and writers have just gotten to the point where they can begin to understand how words work. Often, the phonics and spelling instruction have moved beyond where they need to be, so they never had the chance to learn the critical word strategies they are now ready to learn.

All of the activities in this book are designed to be multilevel—to have something in them at which the whole range of children in a third-grade class can learn and succeed. The activities described include a wide range of things to be learned and, depending on their level, different children will learn different things from the same activity. At the end of this chapter, there is an explanation of how the activities are multilevel and how to "bump them up" or "scale them down" if your class is tilted toward one end or the other of the normal range of third graders. All of the activities stress transfer and application to real reading and writing. For each month, there are suggestions for helping students become more metacognitive, using the strategies when they are needed in actual reading and writing.

Word Wall

The *Word Wall* is the place in the room to put very important words. In third grade, the *Word Wall* contains high-frequency, irregularly spelled words, including common compounds, contractions, and homophones. Also included are words with the most frequently occurring endings, spelling changes, prefixes, and suffixes, so that students have example words for these patterns critical to spelling and decoding polysyllabic words. Though it is impossible to know exactly what words an individual class will need on its *Word Wall*, what follows is a list of 110 words commonly needed on third-grade *Word Walls*.

110 Third Grade Wall Words

The 110 words on the next page are suggested words for use on the *Word Wall* during third grade. The list contains the following:

- the most frequently misspelled words at third-grade level, such as **because**, **they**, **enough**, and **laughed**.

- the most commonly confused homophones, such as **to/too/two**, **write/right,** and **they're/there/their**.

- the most common contractions, such as **they're**, **can't**, **wouldn't**, **I'm**, and **it's**.

- the most common compound words, such as **everybody**, **everything**, **sometimes**, **into**, and **something**.

- a word beginning with each letter, including examples for the **s** sound of **c** (**city**) and the **j** sound of **g** (**general**).

- examples for the common endings and suffixes (**-s**, **-es**, **-ed**, **-ing**, **-ly**, **-er**, **-or**, **-ful**, **-less**, **-ness**, **-en**, **-able**, **-ible**, **-tion**, **-sion**) with common spelling changes (drop **e**, change **y** to **i**, double the final consonant). Examples include **probably**, **especially**, **visually**, **friendly**, **hopeless**, and **laughed**.

- examples for the most common prefixes: **un-**, **re-**, **dis-**, **im-**, **in-** (for example, **discover**, **recycle**, **impossible**, **unhappiness**, **independent**).

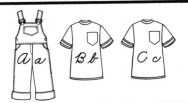

110 *Word Wall* Words for Third Grade

about
again
almost
also
always
another
anyone
are
beautiful
because
before
buy (sell)
by
can't
city
could
community
confusion
countries
didn't
discover
doesn't
don't
enough
especially
everybody
everything
except
exciting
favorite
first
friendly
general
getting
governor
have
hidden

hole (doughnut hole*)
hopeless
I'm
impossible
independent
into
it's (it is)
its
journal
knew
know
laughed
let's
lovable
myself
new (old)
no (yes)
off
one (#1)
our
people
prettier
prettiest
pretty
probably
question
really
recycle
right
said
schools
something
sometimes
terrible
that's
their
then

there (here)
they
they're (they are)
thought
threw (ball*)
through
to
too (also)
trouble
two (#2)
unhappiness
until
usually
vacation
very
want
was
wear (cap*)
weather (cloud*)
went
we're (we are)
were
what
when
where
whether
who
whole
winner
with
won
won't
wouldn't
write (pencil*)
your
you're (you are)

The above list includes homophone clue words in parentheses. These words can be used to give clues to the Word Wall words that sound the same as other words, but have different spellings and meanings. Each clue word should be mounted on the Word Wall next to its corresponding homophone word. The clues marked by an asterisk may be more clearly depicted in illustration form. For example, find a picture of a pencil in a magazine or from an available clip art source, glue the image onto an index card, and place on the Word Wall next to **write**.

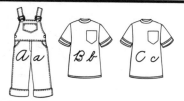 

Each month, words will be suggested for addition to the *Word Wall*. By April, you should have all 110 words displayed. In May/June, lots of review/consolidation activities are suggested so that even the most recalcitrant word learner should be automatically spelling and reading these words by the last day of third grade and (hopefully) on the first day of fourth grade.

Because these words are critical, teachers should have a very high level of expectation for all children learning these words. **Provide a brief, 5-10 minute review activity with the words each day and require students to spell these words correctly in anything they write.** Do not give a spelling test on these words; that would only show if students can spell the words when they are concentrating on them, not if they are using this word knowledge when they need it in reading and writing. To determine if students are learning to spell these words, look at their writing. **In fact, once a word is on the wall, the teacher should hold students "accountable" for that word.** If a student misspells a *Word Wall* word in anything (including a note confiscated as it is being passed to a friend), write "WW" on the word and require the student to fix it! This may sound cruel, but remember that you are trying to help third graders become more responsible and more metacognitive so that they use what they know when they need to use it!

Students who spell **they** as **t-h-a-y** and **said** as **s-e-d**; write **couldn't** without the apostrophe and per-haps missing some letters; and use the wrong **to/too/two** or **right/write** have become automatic at spelling these high-frequency words in the logical way—but unfortunately not the correct way. **The brain has the remarkable ability to make things "automatic" after having processed them several times. Once something is put in the automatic part of the brain, it is carried out without any conscious thought. This automatic-making function of the brain is a wonderful asset when it makes things "automatic right."**

Once a person has had lots of practice driving, she can shift, put on turn signals, steer, etc., while talking to passengers, listening to the radio, or planning dinner. The brain can do many automatic things but only one nonautomatic thing at a time. **When children are just beginning to write, they spell words the logical way: thay, sed, frend.** Because these words are high-frequency, they write them many times, each time spelling them the logical—but wrong—way. After a certain number of times (it varies from brain to brain), the brain assumes this is the correct spelling and puts the spelling in its automatic compartment! **Later, the child learns the correct spellings for they, said, and friend on a spelling list but, because they are only practiced during the week of the test, the child doesn't get enough practice for the brain to decide to replace the spellings in the automatic compart-ment.** When a person is writing, the brain's nonautomatic power is on meaning and except for an occasional new word, the brain's automatic compartment takes care of spelling. When the words in that automatic compartment are correct, this is a marvelous function of the brain; when they are incorrect, we have the often-demonstrated proof that it is not practice that makes perfect, it is perfect practice! (The solution to this problem is not to stop young children from writing until they learn to spell every-thing, but rather to begin a *Word Wall* in first grade and put the irregular high-frequency words on it so that they don't become "automatic wrong"!)

❹ Tell students that **one way to practice words is to say them aloud in a rhythmic chanting fashion.** Tell students that while this might seem silly, it really isn't because **the brain responds to sound and rhythm.** That is one of the reasons students can sing along with the words of a familiar song even though they cannot speak the words without singing the song, and also why jingles and raps are easy to remember.

Point to each word and have students chant it, cheerleader style. Emphasize the "illogical" letters as they chant it. Before "cheering" for each word, help students see what is illogical about it:

again	There are many words whose first syllable begins with an **a** and is pronounced like again (for example, **about, above, ago**). The last syllable is spelled like **rain** and **train**. **Again** used to rhyme with **rain** and **train**.
because	This sounds like it should be spelled **b-e-c-u-z** but is actually logical when you point out the word **cause** and the relationship between **cause** and **because**.
could	There is no explanation for the spelling of **could**. Students may take some consolation in the fact that when they have learned **could**, they can use the same illogical pattern to spell **should** and **would**.
favorite	The word **favor** is spelled logically. Many words that end like **favorite**, such as **definite** and **opposite**, are spelled **ite.**
have	Other **ave** words rhyme with **brave, save,** and **wave**. Hundreds of years ago the word **have** did rhyme with **brave, save,** and **wave**. Its pronunciation has changed but it used to be spelled in a logical way! You might want to have students pronounce **have** the old-fashioned way before cheering its spelling.
into	This is a compound word like **inside** and **infield**.
off	Here is a totally illogical spelling.
people	This is the only word in which it takes **eo** to spell the **e** sound.
said	**Said** should rhyme with **paid** and **braid** and it used to. Pronunciation has changed since the spelling was decided.
they	There is no reason **they** should not be spelled **t-h-a-y**, but it isn't!
until	Where is the double **l** that ends all the other rhyming words?
very	Most rhyming words have two **r**'s (**berry, merry**, etc.).
want	Many **wa** words have a funny pronunciation and follow their own strange **wa** patterns: **was, wad, wash, war, watch, warm, warp**.
who	This is a totally illogical spelling for this word.

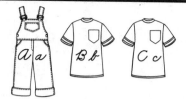 

❺ Once you have discussed what is strange about each word (**visual**), given an explanation when possible, and cheered for each word (**auditory**), have students write each word (**kinesthetic**). **Writing the word with careful attention to each letter and the sequence of letters helps students use another mode to practice the word.** (Do not, however, have students copy words five times each. They just do this "mechanically" and often do not focus on the letters. Sometimes, they copy the words wrong five times, making the automatic wrong spelling ever more automatic!)

Students enjoy writing the words more and focus better on the word if you make it a riddle or game. Do this simply by giving a clue for each word:

Word Wall Riddles

1. Number 1 is the only word with three letters that begins with a vowel.
2. For number 2, write the four-letter word that should be spelled like **say** and **pay**.
3. For number 3, write the four-letter word whose pronunciation used to rhyme with **paid** and **braid**.
4. For number 4, write the four-letter word whose pronunciation used to rhyme with **wave** and **brave**.
5. For number 5, write the four-letter word with the strange **wa** pronunciation.
6. For number 6, write the only word with six letters.
7. For number 7, write the seven-letter word that has the word **cause** in it.

Answer Key: 1. off 2. they 3. said 4. have 5. want 6. people 7. because

---

After students write the words, have them check their own papers by once more chanting the letters aloud, underlining each letter as they say it.

❻ Throughout the month, use the chanting and writing activities (with different clues) for a few minutes each day to practice the words. Occasionally, ask students what is illogical about the spellings of certain words and help them understand the logic that is there (for example, **said** used to rhyme with **paid** and **braid**) when it exists. Many third-grade teachers have students practice handwriting as they practice the *Word Wall* words. They review the printed form of all of the letters for a while and later use the daily *Word Wall* writing time to practice both printing and cursive handwriting.

Most importantly, when students are writing anything, remind them that the wrong spelling of these words is apt to come out of their brains when their attention is on the meaning of what they are writing. If they notice they are writing one of the words displayed, they should stop and glance at the word to get the correct spelling. If they do misspell one of these words, you will help their brains root it out by writing WW on the paper and having them correct the word and turn the paper back in. They won't like this, but if you are relentless they will find themselves thinking "WW" as they incorrectly spell one of these words, thus developing their own self-correction mechanisms!

Using Words You Know

When your students are reading and come to a less frequent word, one they may not have encountered before in reading, what do they do? Good readers who first encounter words, such as **bode**, **spawn**, **swoop**, **inquest**, and **forlorn**, do not hesitate long before coming up with the correct pronunciation. Likewise, when writing, good spellers who need to spell words such as **stress**, **cloak**, or **disgrace** either spell them correctly or in an equally possible way. **Cloak** could be spelled **c-l-o-k-e**. It just isn't! **Disgrace** could be **d-i-s-g-r-a-s-e**. It just isn't!

One clear indicator of a fluent reader and writer is the ability to decode and spell words never seen or used before. Psychologists, who study how our brains process new stimuli, describe the brain as a pattern detector (Caine and Caine, 1991). They explain that when faced with something new, including new words, the brain does a quick search for similar things. For words, these similar things are other words that follow the pattern. **The patterns in one- and two-syllable words are the beginning letters, which linguists call onsets and the rest of the syllable, called rimes.** In **stress**, the onset is **str** and the rime is **ess**. For **cloak**, the onset is **cl** and the rime is **oak**. In **disgrace**, the onset for the first syllable is the **d** and the rime is **is**; for the second syllable the onset is the **gr** and the rime is the **ace**.

Psychologists call the division of new words into onsets and rimes a "psychological reality," which in simple terms means "that's just the way the brain does it!" **This finding that the way the brain deals with words is to look for the pattern, and that the pattern is contained in the onset and rime, is critical to understanding why many children who have been taught phonics rules or to sound words out letter-by-letter are not successful decoders.** The rules lead a reader to break the rime apart as he considers what the **e** on the end might be doing or whether or not the **r** might be controlling the vowel. **Rules explain some of how the phonics system works, but applying rules is not how the brain figures out new words.** In addition to the psychological evidence of the brain looking for patterns and the patterns being the onset and rime, there is firsthand evidence from hordes of poor readers who "know the rules but just don't use them."

So, students who are not using patterns to read and spell words would likely have difficulty reading pattern-following but less-frequent words, such as **bode**, **spawn**, **swoop**, **inquest**, and **forlorn**. They would likely spell words such as **stress**, **cloak**, and **disgrace** in a "put down the sounds you hear" fashion as **stres**, **clok**, and **disgras**. Activities designed to help students learn to decode and spell pattern-following words will not teach them any phonics rules. Rather, the students will learn to decode in a brain-friendly way—using the words they know to decode and spell other words.

In English, words with the same rime usually (but not always!) rhyme. The complication is that some rhymes have two or three different rimes. This is not a problem in decoding an unfamiliar word. When a person is reading the word **cloak** for the first time, the brain will divide it into **cl-** and **-oak** and then use other **-oak** words such as **oak** and **soak** to come up with a pronunciation. When trying to spell cloak, though, the brain does a search for rhyming words and may very well come up with **joke** and **smoke**. Thus, the writer would spell **cloak** following that pattern: **c-l-o-k-e**. Then, if he has ever seen **cloak** before, he might notice it "doesn't look right!" His brain goes looking for other rhymes with a different pattern and may indeed find **oak** and **soak**; he will write that and probably realize, "Now, that looks right!"

The brain has a visual checking system which checks the spelling it generates with what it has seen before. Of course, if the reader has never before seen the word **cloak** in print, there would be no way for your brain's visual checking system to work. That is where the ability to use a dictionary to check the probable spelling of a word plays an important role in good spelling. Later in the year, once students really understand how to spell by pattern, they will learn to use their visual checking system and a dictionary to determine which of two possible patterns is correct through an activity called *What Looks Right?*

Using Words You Know **is designed to help children see that the words they know can help them decode and spell lots of other words.**

How to Do a *Using Words You Know* Lesson [20 min.]

For some words which have lots of rhyming words, this lesson might take two days. For others, the lesson might be completed in one session. **Your students will be more motivated and pay better attention if you spend no more than 20 minutes with a lesson and quit before students are ready to quit!** Below is a sample *Using Words You Know* lesson.

Part 1

❶ **Show students three to five words they know and have them pronounce and spell the words.** For the first lesson, use words of high interest to third graders. Tell students that some of the ways they travel, including **bike**, **car**, **van**, and **train**, can help them spell other words.

❷ **Divide the board, a chart, or a transparency into four columns and head the columns with bike, car, van, and train.** Have each student set up the same columns on a piece of paper and write these four words.

b<u>ike</u>	c<u>ar</u>	v<u>an</u>	tr<u>ain</u>

❸ Remind students that words that rhyme usually have the same spelling pattern. The spelling pattern in a short word begins with the vowel and goes to the end of the word. **Underline the spelling patterns ike, ar, an, and ain,** and have students underline them on their papers.

❹ **Tell students that you are going to show them some words and that they should write them on their papers under the words with the same spelling patterns.** Show them the words below, which you have written on index cards. Let different students go to the board, chart, or transparency and write the words there as the class is writing them on their papers. Do not let the students pronounce the words until they are written on the board. Then, help the students pronounce the words by making them rhyme. Here are some words to use:

pain	Spain	pan	jar	sprain
hike	Fran	spike	than	star

❺ **Explain to students that thinking of rhyming words can also help them spell.** This time, do not show them the words; say the words instead, then have students decide with which word each new word rhymes and use the spelling pattern to spell it. Here are some words you might pronounce and have them spell:

strike	stain	plan	alike	far
strain	bran	brain	scar	Mike

❻ **End this part of the lesson by helping students verbalize that in English, words that rhyme often have the same spelling pattern.** Good readers and spellers don't sound out every letter, rather they try to think of a rhyming word and read or spell the word using the pattern in the rhyming word. The final chart should look like this:

b**ike**	c**ar**	v**an**	tr**ain**
hike	jar	Fran	pain
spike	star	pan	Spain
strike	scar	than	sprain
Mike	far	plan	stain
alike		bran	strain
			brain

Part 2

For the second part of the lesson (probably on the next day), use the same four words and the following procedures:

❶ Head the board, chart, or transparency, and have students head four columns on their papers, with **bike**, **car**, **van**, and **train**. Underline the spelling patterns. **Explain to the students that using the rhyme to help read and spell words works with longer words, too.**

❷ **Show students the words below, written on index cards, and have them write each word in the appropriate column on the chart.** Once each word is written on the board or chart, have students pronounce the word, making the last syllable rhyme:

guitar	motorbike	complain	maintain	orangutan
suntan	dislike	entertain	hitchhike	Superman®

❸ **Now, say each word below. Have students decide with which column the last syllable rhymes and use that spelling pattern to spell the word.** Give help with the spelling of the first part if needed.

Batman®	lifelike	restrain	remain	boxcar
unchain	contain	trashcan	costar	began

❹ **Again, end the lesson by helping students notice how helpful it is to think of a rhyming word they know when trying to read or spell a strange word. The final chart should look like this:**

<u>bike</u>	<u>car</u>	<u>van</u>	<u>train</u>
motorbike	guitar	suntan	complain
dislike	boxcar	Superman®	entertain
hitchhike	costar	Batman®	maintain
lifelike		trashcan	unchain
		began	contain
		orangutan	restrain

In doing *Using Words You Know* **lessons, always choose words students will read and spell.** Don't ask students for rhyming words because, especially for the long vowels, there is often another pattern. **Crane** and **Jane** also rhyme with **train**, but this lesson should only use words that rhyme and have the same pattern. In months to come, when your students are accustomed to reading and spelling by pattern, try some *Reading/Writing Rhymes* and *What Looks Right?* lessons (see pages 52-54 and 93-95) that will help them determine which pattern to use. For now, get them in the habit of seeing words as the onset (all of the letters up to the vowel) and the rime (the spelling pattern).

Dividing words into onsets and rimes is how mature readers and spellers decode and spell; students should break the habit of letter-by-letter decoding and spelling.

All of the *Using Words You Know* lessons work in a similar fashion. Here are the steps:

1. Display and talk about the "words you know."

2. Identify the spelling patterns.

3. Make as many columns as needed on the board, chart, or transparency and on student papers. Head these with the words and underline the spelling patterns.

4. Show students one-syllable words written on index cards and have them write them in the correct columns and use the rhyme to pronounce the words.

5. Say one-syllable words and have students decide how to spell them by deciding with which word they rhyme.

6. Repeat the above procedure with longer words.

7. Help students verbalize how words they know help them read and spell lots of other words, including longer words.

Additional Lessons

Here are three other lessons to help students see how lots of words they know and love will help them decode and spell other words:

Animals that help you read and spell other words:

Words you know:
c<u>at</u>, <u>ape</u>, sn<u>ake</u>, <u>ant</u>

Words to read:
rat, grape, plant, cape, flat, flake, scat, slant, scrape, brake

Words to spell:
shape, chant, drape, chat, grant, wake, brat, tape, splat, shake

Longer words to read:
earthquake, escape, transplant, fruitcake, doormat, acrobat, democrat

Longer words to spell:
combat, enchant, pancake, landscape, mistake, eggplant, nonfat

Foods that help you read and spell other words:

Words you know:

c<u>orn</u>, r<u>ice</u>, m<u>eat</u>, p<u>each</u>

Words to read:

born, beach, treat, slice, preach, worn, wheat, price

Words to spell:

teach, torn, twice, cheat, horn, reach, neat, mice, bleach

Longer words to read:

newborn, impeach, entice, retreat, unicorn, sacrifice, heartbeat

Longer words to spell:

acorn, outreach, device, repeat, backseat, advice, popcorn

Final chart is displayed on page 23.

Names that help you read and spell other words:

Words you know:

J<u>ill</u>, <u>K</u>ate, <u>R</u>ay, <u>M</u>ark

Words to read:

spark, stray, skate, spill, sway, crate, thrill, bark, hill

Words to spell:

late, chill, shark, spray, state, gray, dark, grill

Longer words to read:

yesterday, landmark, whippoorwill, holiday, birthmark, anthill, tailgate, decorate

Longer words to spell:

ballpark, delay, refill, rebate, hibernate, decay, downhill, bookmark

---

Final chart is displayed on page 23.

Using Words You Know
t<u>an</u>... pl<u>an</u>

Animals Chart

<u>c</u>at	<u>ape</u>	sn<u>ake</u>	<u>ant</u>
rat	grape	flake	plant
flat	cape	brake	slant
scat	scrape	wake	chant
chat	shape	shake	grant
brat	drape	earthquake	transplant
splat	tape	fruitcake	enchant
doormat	escape	pancake	eggplant
acrobat	landscape	mistake	
democrat			
combat			
nonfat			

Foods Chart

<u>corn</u>	<u>rice</u>	m<u>ea</u>t	<u>peach</u>
born	slice	treat	beach
worn	price	wheat	preach
torn	twice	cheat	teach
horn	mice	neat	reach
newborn	entice	retreat	bleach
unicorn	sacrifice	heartbeat	impeach
acorn	device	repeat	outreach
popcorn	advice	backseat	

Names Chart

<u>Jill</u>	<u>Kate</u>	<u>Ray</u>	<u>Mark</u>
spill	skate	stray	spark
thrill	crate	sway	bark
hill	late	spray	shark
chill	state	gray	dark
grill	tailgate	yesterday	landmark
whippoorwill	decorate	holiday	birthmark
anthill	rebate	delay	ballpark
refill	hibernate	decay	bookmark
downhill			

Guess the covered word.

Guess the covered word.

Guess the Covered Word

When reading, we recognize most words immediately because we have read them before. We do see new words—words we have never encountered in reading before—and we figure them out. Most words are decoded based on patterns from other words we know. **We also figure out words by combining the context with some of the letter sounds.** Imagine that you are reading the following sentence and the word with just the beginning letters visible is the unfamiliar-in-print word:

The glass overturned and she quickly grabbed a sp⬜ to clean up the mess.

Could you guess the missing word? You know lots of words that begin with **s-p** and if you didn't have the context—the meaning of the rest of the sentence—you would probably have trouble decoding the word **sponge**, which does not follow a pattern from any other words. If you are reading for meaning, however, and if the word **sponge** is in your listening and speaking vocabulary, you will probably identify it immediately in the context of this sentence even if you have never seen it before.

Using the context, all of the initial letters, and word length is not the most efficient way to identify words. It slows down reading because you have to finish the sentence and go back. Combined with a strong base of sight words and the ability to use patterns from familiar words, however, cross checking—using meaning and some letter sounds—is a strategy which helps students identify unfamiliar-in-print words. *Guess the Covered Word* **is an activity which helps students learn to use meaning, word length, and onsets to figure out words.** As students engage in this "captivating" activity, they learn that none of the clues—meaning, beginning letters, or word length—is helpful by itself but together they become a valuable strategy for decoding. Do a couple of *Guess the Covered Word* activities each month to help students become fluent and automatic at cross checking meaning, beginning letters, and word length.

Guess the covered word.

Guess the covered word.

How to Do a *Guess the Covered Word* Activity

20 min.

1. Write some sentences or a paragraph related to something students are studying, or some topic of general interest, on a piece of chart paper.

2. Select one word per sentence which begins with consonant letters and cover that word with two torn self-stick notes. One note should cover all the beginning letters up to the vowel (onset). The other note should cover the rest of the word (rime).

3. Read each sentence aloud and have students make three or four guesses without any letters revealed. Write down these guesses.

4. Remove the note that covers all of the beginning letters. Erase any guesses which are no longer possible. Have students make additional guesses that make sense and have all of the right beginning letters.

5. When the students cannot think of any more words that meet both criteria, reveal the rest of the word and see if the correct word was guessed.

To engage the interest of the students, the first *Guess the Covered Word* lessons should use their names and tell things about them that are positive and interesting. Here is an example. Be sure to use your students' names and interests.

> Ben is a very popular guy.
>
> Justin is a whiz at math.
>
> Karen is one of our super spellers .
>
> David is a champion racer.
>
> Paula loves to read chapter books.
>
> Tyrone is one of our best st▮▮▮▮
>
> Mrs. C. thinks she has a ▮▮▮▮ class.

Making These Activities Multilevel

All three activities described in this chapter are multilevel—they contain multiple things to be learned depending on what various students are ready to learn.

How the *Word Wall* Is Multilevel

Word Wall activities can meet the needs of a wide range of third graders because there are a variety of things to be learned through the short daily practice. Most third graders can read most of these words, but some cannot. The daily *Word Wall* practice provides an avenue for learning to read these critical words. Many third graders have become automatic at spelling some of these words in the "wrong, but logical way." The daily practice and the demand for correct spelling of any *Word Wall* word (any time, any place) will eventually help students to replace the automatic incorrect spelling with an automatic correct spelling. You probably have some students who are already spelling all of these words correctly. For them, the daily practice is a time when they can work on their handwriting—a skill even many precocious third graders need to practice.

You can make the *Word Wall* activity harder or easier by adding the 14 words all at once or by adding them gradually every week or two. You can also make adjustments in the words. High-frequency words such as **here, this**, and **do** have not been included in this book because most third graders spell these words correctly. If, however, you notice frequently written words misspelled by the students in your classroom which are not on the list, you should substitute these for some of the words on the list. Looking at this list and the students' first-draft writing samples should let you know what you need to do. Obviously, if there are some words on this list you know all your students would spell correctly in their writing, you should omit those.

One way to make the *Word Wall* more multilevel is to **help students see how some of the *Word Wall* words can be used to help them spell other words.** The 14 words for the first month were chosen because they are so commonly misspelled by third graders; students don't need any more "wrong practice" to further reinforce the incorrect spellings. Because they are so irregular, the first 14 words do not provide much help with other words. You could help students learn to spell **would** and **should** with the same pattern they are learning in **could** and they should be able to spell **cause** if they can spell **because**. In future months, some suggestions are given for helping students use the *Word Wall* to spell similar words which are not on the wall, thus expanding the usefulness of the *Word Wall* and increasing with little effort the number of words students can spell.

How *Using Words You Know* Is Multilevel

Using Words You Know lessons provide multiple learning possibilities. Most third graders know lots of words—but they often do not use the patterns from those words to read and spell other words. ***Using Words You Know* lessons show them how their words—the words they know—are ready resources for decoding and spelling.** Teachers are amazed at the number of third graders who, after several *Using Words You Know* lessons, finally have the "Aha!" experience. (Sometimes students say, "I never knew you could figure out words this way. I thought you had to sound out each letter.")

Good readers look at each letter but they don't sound out each letter. They look for patterns— large chunks they recognize—and use these much more efficient units. Many third graders who are still slow, labored readers can make incredible progress in reading and spelling if they are in classrooms where they do a lot of reading and writing, and they figure out how to use the raw materials they already have—words they know—to figure out "tons of other words."

Struggling readers can also find things to learn through *Using Words You Know* lessons. **Because of the constant stress on rhyme, they can develop their phonemic awareness if they have not already done so.** Phonemic awareness is also developed as children blend onsets with rimes to read words, and separate onsets from rimes to spell words.

Advanced readers are the major reason that some longer words are included in every *Using Words You Know* **lesson.** Many third graders who would spell **crate** or **slate** correctly would not recognize that they could use that very same pattern to spell the last part of **rebate** or **hibernate**. Third-grade spelling words seldom pose any challenge to the best readers. Persevere with the longer words in *Using Words You Know* lessons and watch them become truly superior decoders and spellers.

How *Guess the Covered Word* Is Multilevel

Guess the Covered Word is another activity with several levels of things to be learned.

Guess the Covered Word helps most third graders consolidate and become automatic at cross checking, a strategy which they may know but often don't use.

For struggling readers, this activity provides practice with all of the beginning letters and teaches them to use all of the letters up to the vowel—not just the first letter.

If the teacher uses words not instantly recognized by most third graders—**fabulous, storyteller, whiz**— the most advanced readers add lots of words to their sight vocabularies through these cross checking lessons. Like the average readers, the advanced readers also become automatic at using this strategy to decode unfamiliar-in-print words.

Applying Strategies When Reading and Writing

In any classroom, the majority of time available for language arts should be devoted to actual reading and writing. The decoding and spelling strategies described in this book will only be helpful to students if they are reading and writing every day and beginning to employ these strategies as they read and write. **Here are some "reminders" teachers can say to students as they begin a reading or writing activity:**

Before Writing:

"As you are writing, concentrate your attention on what you are trying to say—the meaning or message you want to get across. When you finish writing, but before putting your piece away for the day, reread it. Look for any *Word Wall* words that you spelled in the old, logical but wrong, way. Correct these immediately. Look for other words which don't look right to you. Do you know a rhyming word that might have the same spelling pattern? Write it that way and see if it looks right."

After Writing:

"Tell me some examples of *Word Wall* words you fixed in your writing today and/or words that didn't look right to you and for which you tried a different pattern. I am pleased to see that all of you are monitoring your spelling and applying what you have been learning during spelling lessons."

Before Reading:

"All readers come to words they have heard but have never before seen in print. When you come to an unfamiliar word, stop and say all of the letters in that word. Don't try to sound out each letter, just spell the word to yourself, naming the letters. This allows your brain to search through all its stored words and see if you know a word with the same pattern that will help you figure out the new word. If you come up with a probable pronunciation based on some similar words, try it out and see if it makes sense with what you are reading. Remember that "guessing" a word just based on the meaning, or just on the first letters, or just on word length won't work very well. When you combine all three as we do in *Guess the Covered Word* lessons, though, you can make a good guess if the word is one you have heard before."

(You may want to give self-stick notes to the students as they begin to read and ask them to write any words they figure out for themselves.)

After Reading:

Give me some examples of words you figured out by saying all of the letters; looking in your word stores for words with similar patterns; or by using meaning, onset, and word length. Did you write any words on your self-stick note? If so, would you please come write your words on the board and explain the decoding strategies you used to the rest of the class?

Remember, third graders know more than they use. One of the big third-grade hurdles is to start students automatically using their strategies when they need them.

Month at a Glance

For most teachers, when you get to October, you feel like you "might" make it through the year! By now your students should be into the "routines" for your classroom. You can begin to make some progress.

This month, we cover the following:
- expanding the *Word Wall* by adding 14 more words
- introducing extensions to other words involving doubling consonants, **y** to **i** spelling change, dropping the final e before endings, and Spelling Change Banners
- *Using Words You Know* lessons that change the vowel in the spelling patterns **at**, **et**, **it**, **ot**, and **ut**
- *Guess the Covered Word* opportunities in paragraph form
- introducing an activity called *Making Words*

Here are some time guidelines to consider this month:

Class with Most Children On Grade Level
- 5 minutes *Word Wall* practice daily
- Three 20-minute word lessons each week, including *Using Words You Know, Making Words,* and *Guess the Covered Word*

Class with Most Children Struggling with Grade-Level Material
- 10 minutes *Word Wall* practice daily
- One 20-minute word lesson every day, including *Using Words You Know, Making Words,* and *Guess the Covered Word*

Class with Almost All Children On or Above Grade Level
- 5 minutes *Word Wall* practice daily
- Two 20-minute word lessons each week, picking and choosing from *Using Words You Know, Making Words,* and *Guess the Covered Word*

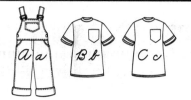 
Word Wall

10 min.

If you have been providing cheering and writing practice, reminding students to check their writing for *Word Wall* words, and returning papers with WW's on them, most of your students should have learned correct spellings for last month's words. This month's words include more commonly misspelled words, along with the most commonly misspelled homophones, examples for the two sounds of **c**, and lots of examples for endings and spelling changes. Here are the words for this month:

city	community	countries	exciting	getting	pretty	prettier
prettiest	laughed	schools	to	too	two	was

As you work with these and future words, follow these procedures:

❶ **Add the words to your display.** Put the word **was** on a different color from last month's word **want**. Use different colors for **to**, **two**, and **too**. In addition, attach a clue such as **#2** to the word **two** and the word **also** to the word **too**.

The *Word Wall* now shows August/September words with the new October words. If you are also using the portable *Word Walls*, give students a new sheet to which the new words (and clues) have been added (see page 155 for a reproducible).

❷ **Focus student attention on each word** and have students chant it, cheerleader style. Before "cheering" for each word, point out any helpful patterns and anything illogical about the word:

city	Point out the **s** sound of **c**. Help students think of other words they know in which the **s** sound is spelled with the letter **c** (for example, **cent**, **citrus**, **cereal**, **circus**, **bicycle**).
community	Help students cheer this word in chunks—**com-mun-ity**. Help them see that the first part start lots of words they know (**company**, **comfortable**, **committee**). The last part—**ity**—is the same rime as **city**.
countries	Help students see that **countries** is the plural of **country**. Have them spell **country** and notice that it ends in **y** like **city** and **community**. Tell them that the beginning part is spelled like **count** but pronounced a little differently. Explain one spelling rule students can always depend on: if a word ends in **y**, the **y** is changed to **i** and **-es** is added to make it plural.
exciting	**Exciting** is actually spelled logically but, since many people pronounce it as "eg-ziting," it just seems illogical! Have students notice the **s** sound for **c** and that the final **e** is dropped when **-ing** is added.
getting	The **t** is doubled before **-ing** is added. This word is spelled like **betting** and **petting**, although often pronounced like **sitting** and **spitting**.
laughed	This is **laugh** with the ending **-ed**. There is no reason for **laugh** to be spelled in this funny, "laughable" way. Notice that it sounds like a **t** at the end but is spelled with an **-ed**.
schools	Here is **school** with the **s** ending. There is no logical explanation for the **h**.
to/two/too	Have students notice the clues you attached to two of these. For **two**, point out the related words **twin** and **twice**, which also begin with **tw**. For the "also" **too**, have students pronounce the word emphasizing the **oo**: "She is here, too—oo—oo." Tell them that when they find themselves writing this word, they should ask themselves if it is the number 2 or the "also" **too**. If it is neither of these, they should use one with no clue—**to**. As you have them cheer for these, they should also say each clue:

"t-o—to; t-w-o—number 2; t-o-o—also"

pretty/prettier/prettiest	**Pretty** is often pronounced to rhyme with **bitty** but spelled like **Betty**. Talk about the **-er** (meaning "more") and **-est** (meaning "most") endings, and how once again the **y** changes to an **i** before **-er** and **-est** are added.
was	This is one of those **wa** words like **want**. **S** at the end of words often sounds like **z**, as in **is**, **has**, and **does**.

❸ **Use writing clues to have students write each word.** Make sure that your clues distinguish these words from each other and from last month's words. Here are some possibilities:

Word Wall Riddles

1. Number 1 is the word that must have a letter doubled before adding **-ing**.

2. For number 2, write the four-letter word that has the **s** sound for **c**.

3. For number 3, write the word that has an ending meaning "more."

4. For number 4, write the word that has an ending meaning "most."

5. For number 5, write the word that begins with **t** and is a number.

6. For number 6, write the word that begins with **t** and means "also."

7. For number 7, write the other word that is pronounced just like the words you wrote for 5 and 6.

Answer Key: 1. **getting** 2. **city** 3. **prettier** 4. **prettiest** 5. **two** 6. **too** 7. **to**

After students write the words, have them check their own papers by once more chanting the letters aloud, underlining each letter as they say it.

On the day new words are added, practice only the new words. Throughout the month, however, use the chanting and writing activities (with different clues) to practice all of the words. **Do not do more than seven words on any one day**, but mix them up so that students are continually practicing all of the words. Occasionally, ask students what is illogical about the spelling of certain words and help them understand the logic when it exists. When students are writing anything from now on, they should be held accountable for all 28 words on the *Word Wall*. If they use the wrong **to/too/two**, write "WW" next to it and let them use the clues to figure out which one was needed.

Extending the *Word Wall* to Other Words

Once students are good at spelling the 28 words on your wall, they should begin using the patterns that exist to spell other words. From last month, they should realize that **could** will help them spell **should** and **would** and that the word **cause** is in the word **because**. Review these and then **show students how the endings and spelling changes can help them spell other words.** Have students spell the following words, explain how the *Word Wall* helps spell them, and talk about spelling changes needed:

should	would	cause	cities	communities	country
excite	excited	get	laugh	laughing	school

On other days, take common words students can spell and have them practice spelling these words with endings. Give them some examples such as these:

- If you can spell **happy**, **funny**, and **smelly**, how would you spell **happier**, **happiest**, **funnier**, **funniest**, **smellier**, and **smelliest**?

- If you can spell **baby**, **puppy**, and **mommy**, how would you spell **babies**, **puppies**, and **mommies**?

- If you can spell **bake**, **skate**, and **hope**, how would you spell **baking**, **skating**, and **hoping**?

- If you can spell **hit**, **cut**, and **bat**, how would you spell **hitting**, **cutting**, and **batting**?

Have a Contest and Make Spelling Change Banners

Kids love contests and banners. Put students in teams of three or four, give them one of the ending/spelling change patterns, such as "**y** to **i** and add **es**," and have them see how many words that follow that pattern they can list in five minutes. Use a timer and let the winning team write their list with brightly colored markers on a "**y** to **i** and add **es**" banner. When the banner is finished, let other teams add their examples which were not included by the winning team. On other days, have contests and banners for "**y** to **i** and add **er/est**," "drop **e**, add **-ing**," and "double the **t**." (Point out to students that only words that end in the single consonant **t** double the **t**.)

y to i and add es

babies   cherries   pennies   butterflies   stories   berries
bunnies   puppies   daisies   buddies   countries   families
ponies   cities   parties   ladies

Making Words

20 min.

Making Words **is another activity which accomplishes the same goals as** *Using Words You Know*. Students learn that there are patterns in words, that a little change in the letters of a word changes it in a predictable way, and that words can be sorted into patterns and then used to read and spell other words. See page 36 for a sample *Making Words* lesson.

To plan a *Making Words* lesson, do the following:

1. Begin with a "secret" word—a word which can be made from all of the letters you will use.

2. Using the letters in the secret word, choose 12-15 words which will give some easy and some harder words and several sets of rhymes.

3. Decide on the order in which words will be made, beginning with short words and building to longer words. Write these words on index cards to use in the sorting and transferring parts of the lesson.

4. Write the letters on a strip—vowels first, then consonants, so as not to give away the secret word. (Reproducible strips for all of the lessons in this book are found on pages 162-169.)

5. To begin the lesson, give students the strips, have them write the matching uppercase letters on the back, and let them cut or tear the strips into individual letters.

6. Place large letter cards with the same letters along the chalk ledge or in a pocket chart.

7. As students make each word, choose one student to come and make it with the big letters.

8. After all of the words have been made, have students sort by patterns such as beginning sounds, rhyming words, prefixes, plurals, etc.

9. After all of the words have been sorted, remind students that rhyming words can help them read and spell other words. Show two new rhyming words to students and have them use the rhymes to decode the new words. Then, say two new rhyming words and have students use the rhymes to spell the new words.

Example Lesson: Make

1 The secret word for this lesson is **Titanic**. As the lesson begins, the letters **a, i, i, c, n, t,** and **t** are in the pocket chart. The students have the same letters. The teacher leads them to make words by saying the following:

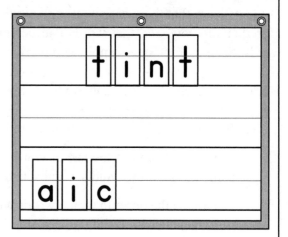

a. "Take two letters and make **at**."

b. "Change the vowel to make the word **it**."

c. "Change **it** into **in**."

d. "Now, we are going to make some three-letter words. Add one letter to **in** to spell **tin**."

e. "Just change the vowel in **tin** and you will have **tan**."

f. "Rearrange the letters and spell **ant**."

g. "Change just one letter and you can spell **act**."

h. "Rearrange the letters again and spell **cat**."

i. "Change just one letter and turn your **cat** into a **can**."

j. "Now, let's make some four-letter words. Use four letters to spell **tint**. A **tint** is just a little bit of color. Carol's hair has a **tint** of red in it. Everyone say **tint**. Stretch it out and think about the letters you hear."

k. "Now, spell another four-letter word, **tact**. Some people don't have any **tact**. They just say what they think, even if it hurts someone's feelings. Everyone say **tact**."

l. "Now, let's make some five-letter words. Use five of your letters to spell **attic**. Make sure you use five letters."

m. "Change just one letter in **attic** and you can spell **antic**. The teacher told the boy to stop that silly **antic**."

n. "I have one six-letter word for you to spell: **intact**. If we leave something together, we leave it **intact**. After the tornado struck, only the school cafeteria was **intact**. Everyone say **intact**. Stretch it out and listen to the letters you are saying."

o. "Every *Making Words* lesson has a secret word—a word than can be made with all of the letters. Take a minute and see if anyone can figure out the secret word. It is a tricky word. If no one can figure it out in a minute, I will give you some clues."

2 If someone figures out **Titanic**, the teacher lets that student come and make it with the big letters. If not, she gives them some clues ("It's the name of a ship." "It sunk many years ago." "Several movies have been made about it.") When they figure it out, the teacher has all students make the word—using their uppercase **t**—and lets someone come and make it with the big letters.

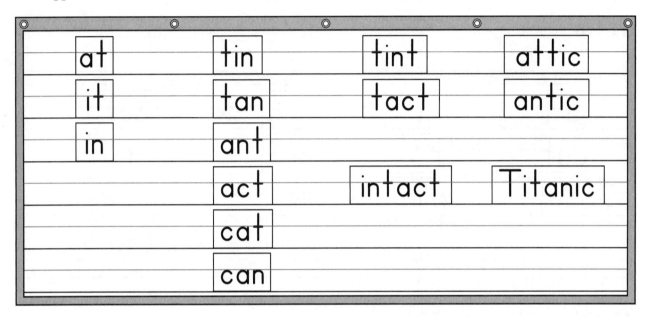

Sort:

3 **Once all of the words are made, the teacher leads the students to sort for patterns.** For the sorting part of the lesson, she puts the words on index cards in the pocket chart or along the chalk ledge. In this lesson, she first sorts out the three words that end in **ic**; points out that **attic**, **antic**, and **Titanic** are all spelled with **ic** at the end; and notes that the ending syllable for each has the same pronunciation. Next, the class sorts the words into rhymes:

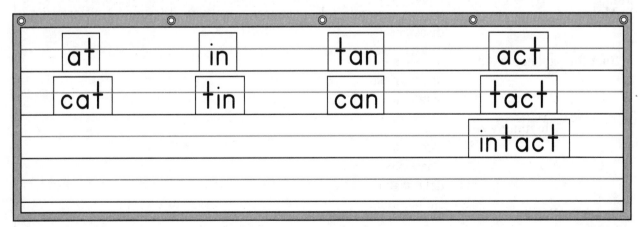

4 **Transfer Step: When the rhyming words are sorted, the teacher reminds the students that rhyming words can help them read and spell words.** She then writes two new rhyming words, **fact** and **plan**, on cards, has students place these words under the rhyming words, and lets students use the rhymes to decode them.

5 Finally, the teacher says two rhyming words, **chat** and **thin**, and helps students see how the words they made help spell the new words.

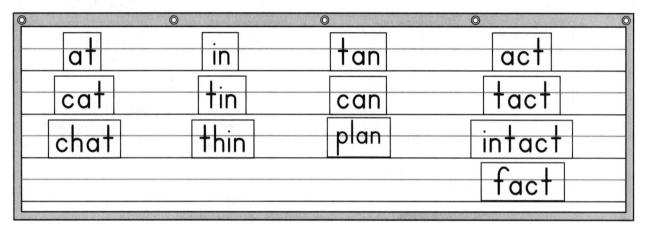

Additional Lessons

Here are two other *Making Words* lessons for this month. (The **/** indicates a word that can be turned into another word by rearranging the same letters.)

Lesson Two:	**Secret Word: disaster**
Letters on strip:	a e i d r s s t
Make:	tie, die, dies/side, tide, dear, tear, tears/stare, dries, driest, sister/resist, disaster
Sort for: related words:	die, dies dries, driest tear, tears
rhyming words:	tie, die side, tide dries, dies dear, tear
Transfer Words:	clear, lie, pies, bride

Lesson Three:	Secret Word: unsinkable
Letters on strip:	a e i u b k l n n s
Make:	us, use, Sal, seal, sane, lane, able, sink, blink, insane, usable, unable, unseal, unsinkable
Sort for: related words:	sane, insane
-able words:	usable, unsinkable
un- opposites:	unable, unseal, unsinkable
rhyming words:	sane, lane, insane
	sink, blink
Transfer Words:	think, crane, stink, shrink

Making Words is lots of fun if you keep it fast paced. Approximately 15 words should be made in no more than 15 minutes. Take another 6-8 minutes for sorting and transferring and you are finished while students are still eager to make other words with the letters.

At the end of the school day, give students another copy of the same letter strip used for the lesson done in class. Have them write uppercase letters on the back before leaving school. Their homework assignment is to see how many words they can make from the letters. Often the whole family gets into the *Making Words* homework game. Some families get very competitive about figuring out the secret word, and their child, who did the lesson in class, is the only one who knows it!

There is a book available with lessons teachers can use for home or school: *Making Words Lessons for Home or School (Grade 3)* by Cunningham and Hall (Carson-Dellosa, 2001).

Using Words You Know

20 min.

This month's *Using Words You Know* lessons review the short vowel sounds and focus student attention on how the vowel sounds change in spelling patterns that are the same except for the vowel.

The steps of this month's first *Using Words You Know* lesson are as follows:

Part One

❶ Show students the words **cat**, **bet**, **sit**, **hot**, and **but**, written on the board or index cards. Have students pronounce and spell the words.

❷ Divide the board, a chart, or a transparency into five columns and head the columns with **cat**, **bet**, **sit**, **hot**, or **but**. Have students set up the same columns on a piece of paper and write these five words.

❸ Remind students that words which rhyme usually have the same spelling pattern. Explain that the spelling pattern in a short word begins with the vowel and goes to the end of the word. Underline the spelling patterns **at**, **et**, **it**, **ot**, and **ut**, and have students underline them on their papers. Help students to notice that what makes the spelling pattern in these words different is only the vowel. They will have to look closely at the words you show them and listen carefully to the words you say so that they can decide which vowel to use.

❹ Tell students that you will show them some words and that they should write them in the column with the same spelling pattern. Show them the words below, which you have written on index cards. Let different students go to the board, chart, or transparency and write the words there as the rest of the students are writing them on their papers. Do not let the students pronounce the words until they are written on the board. Then, help the students pronounce the words by making them rhyme. Here are some words to use:

yet	spit	clot	vat	hut
cut	net	flat	strut	knot

❺ Remind students that thinking of rhyming words can also help them spell. This time you will not show them the words; you will say words. Students will have to decide with which word each rhymes and use that spelling pattern to spell the word. Here are some words you might pronounce and have students spell:

shut	fat	slot	quit	glut
split	wet	plot	shot	vet

6 End this part of the lesson by reminding students that, in English, words that rhyme often have the same spelling pattern. Good readers and spellers don't sound out every letter. They try to think of a rhyming word and read or spell the unfamiliar word using the pattern in the rhyming word.

Part Two

For the second part of the lesson (probably on the next day), use these procedures:

1 Set up columns on the board, chart, or transparency, and have students set up five columns on their papers, with the words **cat**, **bet**, **sit**, **hot**, and **but**. Underline the spelling patterns. Explain to the students that using the rhyme to help read and spell unfamiliar words also works with longer words.

2 Show students the following words written on index cards and have them write the words in the appropriate columns. Once a word is written on the board or chart, have students pronounce the word, making the last syllable rhyme with the other words in the column:

clarinet	commit	alphabet	nitwit	quartet
mascot	wombat	coconut	chestnut	robot

3 Now say the following words. For each, have students decide with which word the last syllable rhymes and use that spelling pattern to spell it. Give help with the spelling of the first part if needed.

jackpot	permit	upset	shortcut	reset
diplomat	forgot	armpit	format	wildcat

4 Again, end the lesson by helping students notice how helpful it is to think of a familiar rhyming word when trying to read or spell a strange word. The final chart should look like this:

c<u>at</u>	b<u>et</u>	s<u>it</u>	h<u>ot</u>	b<u>ut</u>
flat	yet	spit	clot	cut
vat	net	quit	knot	strut
fat	wet	split	slot	hut
wombat	vet	commit	plot	shut
diplomat	clarinet	nitwit	shot	coconut
format	alphabet	permit	mascot	chestnut
wildcat	quartet	armpit	robot	shortcut
	upset		jackpot	
	reset		forgot	

All the *Using Words You Know* lessons work in a similar fashion. These are the steps:

1. Display and talk about the words.

2. Identify the spelling patterns.

3. Make as many columns as needed on the board, chart, or transparency and on student papers. Head these with the words and underline the spelling patterns.

4. Show students one-syllable words written on index cards. Have them write each word in the column showing the same pattern and use the rhyme to pronounce the word.

5. Say one-syllable words and have students decide how to spell them by deciding with which word they rhyme.

6. Repeat the above procedure with longer words.

7. Help students verbalize how words they know help them read and spell lots of other words, including longer words.

Additional Lesson

Here is another lesson which allows you to work with the sounds of all five vowels:

Words you know:
   bl<u>ack</u>, n<u>eck</u>, s<u>ick</u>, r<u>ock</u>, tr<u>uck</u>

Words to read:
   struck, shock, yuck, stock, stick, stuck, stack, wreck, whack

Words to spell:
   stuck, clock, click, muck, check, smock, speck, snack, smack

Longer words to read:
   woodchuck, yardstick, roadblock, peacock, homesick, livestock, racetrack, shipwreck

Longer words to spell:
   unlock, shamrock, paycheck, seasick, padlock, toothpick, raincheck, backpack, lipstick

Guess the covered word.

Guess the covered word.

Guess the Covered Word

20 min.

Remember to provide practice with cross checking by occasionally giving students some sentences or a paragraph in which they have to guess some words, first with no letters showing and then with all of the letters up to the vowel showing. Students should become good at using meaning, beginning letters, and word length to figure out words. Here is an example based on an event which interests most third graders: Halloween, told from a teacher's memories of the "good old days":

Remembering Halloween

When I was your age I **loved** Halloween. We had parties at school and we all came dressed up in **strange** costumes. Most of these costumes were **homemade** . Sometimes there was a costume **contest** . We had **scrumptious** cookies. My mother used to send **baked** apples. Halloween night, when it was **pitch** dark, we went trick-or-treating. We each carried a **flashlight** and stayed together in a group. Most people were very nice to us but some people **scowled** at us. There was one house we never visited because it was **haunted** . In those days, we didn't have **much** candy. I divided my candy so that it would last until **Thanksgiving** .

Making These Activities Multilevel

Think about this month's activities and how they can stretch to meet the range of reading and writing levels in your classroom.

How the *Word Wall* Is Multilevel

Many of the *Word Wall* words for this month give examples for common spelling changes. Even the most advanced third graders often do not consistently change **y**'s to **i**'s, drop **e**'s, and double **t**'s when needed. Providing an example on the *Word Wall* and then practicing with similar words will help even the best readers and writers move forward in spelling.

How *Making Words* Is Multilevel

Making Words activities are multilevel in a number of ways:

- **The activities always begin with some short, easy words so that third graders who have not yet figured out the system can see how small changes change words.**

- As the lesson continues, **the words get bigger and more complex**. A few words not commonly known by many third graders are included. **There are sentence examples and meanings for these, and this helps enlarge the vocabularies of more advanced students.**

- **Figuring out the secret word is often a challenge to even the most advanced readers.**

- **As they sort the words by patterns, different children will notice different things.** Not all third graders will understand how **unusable**, **unseal**, and **unsinkable** are alike and related to the root words, but many will.

- When students stretch out words and sort for rhymes, they are once again **improving phonemic awareness**.

- The transfer words help all children **use words they know to decode and spell other words**.

How *Using Words You Know* Is Multilevel

Again this month, the *Using Words You Know* lessons provide multiple learning possibilities:

- Some children are beginning to understand how lots of words they know—not just the ones you have covered in class—will help them decode and spell other words.

- Other children needed this review of short vowel patterns and may be beginning to understand how words change with the different vowels.

- For children whose literacy is just developing, the instruction on beginning sounds, blending these onsets with rimes to read words, and segmenting onsets from rimes develops phonemic awareness and is critical to spell words.

- Your terrific readers should be developing some big-word spelling skills which are beyond those normally taught in third grade.

How *Guess the Covered Word* Is Multilevel

Do your students like *Guess the Covered Word*? Many teachers tell us that this is the "hands down" favorite word activity. **Be sure to include some less common words (for example, *scowled*, *scrumptious*) to keep your best readers on their toes.**

Applying Strategies When Reading and Writing

Remember to stress to students that they are "third graders now" and they are becoming more independent and responsible—more grown up! Help them to see that some of the things you are doing with words are moving them toward that goal. The *Word Wall* is there so that they can spell these "pesky" words like the grown-ups do and they don't have to ask anyone. There are also helpful examples on the *Word Wall* to help them remember the spelling changes they need when adding certain endings.

As students are preparing to read, remind them that **since they are third graders now, what they are reading is going to be more grown-up and "sophisticated." They will meet more unfamiliar words than they did when they were in earlier grades reading "easy" books.** Have them see meeting an unfamiliar word as an indication of their "grown-up-ness" rather than as a sign of failure. Ask them what they will do when they come to unfamiliar words. Have them explain in their own words how they will use patterns and cross checking. Remind them to always check their pronunciation to make sure it makes sense and "sounds right."

*Charts shown are from Carson-Dellosa's *Word Wall "Plus" for Third Grade* (CD-2504).

When you are reading with a small group or individual child, coach them to use their strategies instead of telling them the words:

1. When a child comes to an unknown word and looks up at you, say, "Put your finger on the word and say all of the letters."

2. Many times, after saying the letters, the child will correctly pronounce the word. Acknowledge the good strategy the child is using by saying something like, "Terrific. That's what good readers do. They meet lot of words they don't immediately recognize but they look at all of the letters and can often figure them out."

3. If the child does not correctly pronounce the word after saying all of the letters, say, "Keep your finger there so you can get right back to that word, then finish the sentence."

4. Often, after finishing the sentence and looking back, especially if you have been doing *Guess the Covered Word* activities, the child will pronounce the word correctly. **Be sure to point out the strategy used:** "See. You didn't know the word but when you finished the sentence and thought about what makes sense, begins with all of the right letters, and is about the right length, you could figure it out."

5. If the child cannot figure out the word after reading the sentence, give a pattern clue: "Let's see, the word is spelled **m-u-n-c-h**. You know what **l-u-n-c-h** spells. Can you make this word begin with an **m** and rhyme with **lunch**?"

6. Sometimes, the context or pattern is not helpful, but there is something in the picture a good reader would have noticed to help with that word: "That's a hard word to figure out but do you recognize the kind of tree the girl is standing under. We have them here, too. It's a big tree whose name starts with an **m**, and it is a fairly long word. Yes, she is standing under a **magnolia** tree. Sometimes, the picture can help us with unusual words."

This kind of "when needed" coaching, along with all of the good words activities you are doing, should help even the most resistant third grader start using the word strategies when needed.

Month at a Glance

By now, you should be thankful that all students are more conscientiously using what they know about words, in both their reading and their writing. Consistency is paying off! Chanting and cheering words has replaced misspelled words with correct spellings.

This month, the following activities will be suggested:

- expanding the *Word Wall* by adding 14 more words, including extensions to other words involving prefixes and suffixes
- *Using Words You Know* lessons that review long vowel sounds and focus on patterns, such as **ate**, **ete**, **ite**, **ote**, and **ute**, that are the same except for the vowel
- *Guess the Covered Word* in paragraph form, extended to social studies
- *Making Words* lessons related to the social studies theme of community
- introducing *Reading/Writing Rhymes*, an activity for pattern decoding and spelling using **and** and **ent**

Here are some time guidelines to consider this month:

Class with Most Children On Grade Level

- 5 minutes *Word Wall* practice daily
- Three 20-minute word lessons each week, including *Reading/Writing Rhymes, Using Words You Know, Making Words,* and *Guess the Covered Word*

Class with Most Children Struggling with Grade-Level Material

- 10 minutes *Word Wall* practice daily
- One 20-minute word lesson every day, including *Reading/Writing Rhymes, Using Words You Know, Making Words,* and *Guess the Covered Word*

Class with Almost All Children On or Above Grade Level

- 5 minutes *Word Wall* practice daily
- Two 20-minute word lessons each week, picking and choosing from *Reading/Writing Rhymes, Using Words You Know, Making Words,* and *Guess the Covered Word*

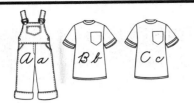

Word Wall

10 min.

It is a new month and time to learn 14 more important words! Here are the words for this month:

beautiful	before	discover	enough	first	hopeless	journal
let's	recycle	their	there	they're	went	when

❶ Add the words to your display. **When adding words that begin with the same letter, use different colors. Use different colors for there, their, and they're. Attach a card saying "they are" next to they're and underline the h-e-r-e in there.** If you are also using the portable *Word Walls*, give students a new sheet to which the new words (and clues) have been added (see page 156 for a reproducible).

❷ Focus student attention on each word and have students chant it cheerleader-style. Emphasize the "illogical" letters as they chant. Before "cheering" for each word, help students see what is illogical about it:

beautiful	This is the word **beauty** with the **y** changed to **i** before adding **-ful**. Other common **-ful** words include **useful** and **helpful**.
before	This is actually spelled logically because the **fore** is related to words like **forehead** and **forecast**, not **for**. Point out that it begins with the same "chunk" as **because**.
discover	**Discover** is the word **cover** with the prefix **dis-**. **Dis-** is a common prefix which often changes a word to an opposite meaning. You **cover** something to hide it. When you **discover** it, it is no longer hidden or covered. Other common **dis-** words in which **dis-** means "the opposite" include **dishonest** and **disobey**.
enough	Again, there is no explanation for the spelling of the last syllable, but once you can spell it you can also spell **rough** and **tough**!
first	This is quite logical but for some unknown reason often misspelled **f-r-i-s-t**!
hopeless	Here is the word **hope** with the suffix **-less,** meaning "without." Other common **-less** words include **useless** and **helpless**.
journal	This is an example for the letter **j** ending in the common spelling pattern **al**.
let's	This is a contraction for **let us**. The apostrophe replaces the **u**. When you cheer for this, make a clicking sound and gesture for the apostrophe.

recycle   This is the word **cycle** with the common prefix **re-,** meaning "back" or "again." Other common **re-** words include **return** and **replace**. **Recycle** has both sounds for the letter **c** and ends in the common **le** pattern just like **people**.

there/their/   Have students notice the clues you attached to two of these. For the word **there**,
they're   explain that you underlined the **here** because this is the word that often means the opposite of **here**.

"I was not **here**—I was **there**. **Here** it is—**there** it is."

They're is a contraction for **they are**. Tell students that when they find themselves writing this word, they should ask themselves if it is the opposite of **here** or if they could write "they are." If it is neither of these, they should use one with no clue: **their**. As you have them cheer for these, they should also say the clue and make a clicking sound and gesture for the apostrophe in **they're**.

"t-h-e-i-r—their; t-h-e-r-e—there/here; t-h-e-y-'-r-e—they're/they are"

went/when   These are not illogical but often misspelled **w-i-n-t** and **w-i-n**, especially if pronounced like that.

❸ Use writing clues to have students write the words. Make sure that the clues distinguish these words from each other and from last month's words. Here are some possibilities:

Word Wall Riddles

1. Number 1 is the only word on the *Word Wall* that begins with **j**.

2. For number 2, write the word whose last syllable rhymes with and is spelled like **rough** and **tough**.

3. For number 3, write the eight-letter word that means "without hope."

4. For number 4, write the six-letter word that begins with **be.**

5. For number 5, write the word that begins with **th** and is the opposite of **here**.

6. For number 6, write the word that begins with **th** and is a contraction.

7. For number 7, write the other word that is pronounced just like the words you wrote for 5 and 6.

Answer Key: 1. **journal** 2. **enough** 3. **hopeless** 4. **before** 5. **there** 6. **they're** 7. **their**

After students write the words, have them check their own papers by once more chanting the letters aloud, underlining each letter as they say it.

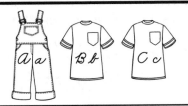

As the month goes on, use the chanting and writing activities to practice all 42 words. **Do not do more than seven on any one day, but mix them up so that students are continually practicing all of the words.** Occasionally, ask students what is illogical about the spelling of certain words and help them understand the logic that is there when it exists. Review all endings and spelling changes. Have students point out suffixes and prefixes and talk about their meanings. When students are writing anything from now on, they should be held accountable for all 42 words. If they use the wrong **to/too/two** or **there/their/they're**, write "WW" next to it and let them use the clues to figure out which one was needed.

Extending the *Word Wall* to Other Words

Once students are proficient at spelling the 42 words on your wall, they should begin using the patterns to spell other words. From last month, they should realize that they can spell these words:

should	**would**	**cause**	**cities**	**communities**	**country**
excite	**excited**	**get**	**laugh**	**laughing**	**school**

In addition, students should now be able to spell the following words:

beauty	**cover**	**covers**	**covered**	**covering**
recover	**recovers**	**recovered**	**recovering**	**discovers**
discovered	**discovering**	**rough**	**tough**	**hope**
hopes	**hoped**		**hoping**	**hopeful**

To further extend the *Word Wall* lessons, take common words students can spell and have them practice spelling these words with prefixes and suffixes. Give them some examples such as these:

- If you can spell **turn**, **place**, and **port**, how would you spell **return**, **replace**, and **report**?

- If you can spell **count**, **prove**, and **like**, how would you spell **discount**, **disprove**, and **dislike**?

- If you can spell **use**, **end**, and **care**, how would you spell **useless**, **endless**, and **careless**?

- If you can spell **help**, **joy**, and **thank**, how would you spell **helpful**, **joyful**, and **thankful**?

If your students enjoyed listing spelling change examples with endings and making banners (see page 34), you might do this again with the suffixes **-ful** and **-less**.

Reading/Writing Rhymes

20 min.

Reading/Writing Rhymes **is another activity which helps students learn to use patterns to decode and spell hundreds of words. In addition, all initial sounds (onsets) are reviewed every time you do a** *Reading/Writing Rhymes* **lesson.** Once all of the rhyming words are generated on a chart, students write rhymes using these words and then read each other's rhymes. Because writing and reading are connected to every lesson, students learn to use these patterns as they actually read and write.

Here is how to do *Reading/Writing Rhymes* lessons:

❶ Create an Onset Deck containing cards for all of the beginning sounds. The cards, 3" x 5" index cards, are laminated and have the single-letter consonants written in blue, the blends in red, and the digraphs and other two-letter combinations in green. On one side of each card, the first letter of the onset is a uppercase letter. On the other side, the entire onset is lowercase. The onset deck contains 50 beginning letter cards:

Single consonants:	b, c, d, f, g, h, j, k, l, m, n, p, r, s, t, v, w, y, z
Digraphs (two letters, one sound):	sh, ch, wh, th
Other two-letter, one-sound combinations:	kn, qu
Blends (beginning letters blended together, sometimes called clusters)	bl, br, cl, cr, dr, fl, fr, gl, gr, pl, pr, sc, scr, sk, sl, sm, sn, sp, spl, spr, st, str, sw, tr, tw

At the beginning of the lesson, distribute all of the onset cards to the students. Depending on the class, you may distribute them to individual children or to teams of two or three children.

❷ Once all of the onset cards are distributed, write the spelling pattern with which you are working 10-12 times on a piece of chart paper. As you write it each time, have the children help spell it and pronounce it. For this example, the spelling pattern is **and.**

❸ Next, **a**sk if anyone has a card he thinks will make a word when combined with **and**. Allow one student to come up, place his card next to one of the written spelling patterns, and pronounce the word. If the word is real, use the word in a sentence and write that word on the chart. If the word is not real, explain why it cannot be written on the chart. (If a word is real and does rhyme but has a different spelling pattern, such as **planned** to rhyme with **and**, explain that it rhymes but has a different pattern and include it on the bottom of the chart with an asterisk next to it.) Write names with uppercase initial letters. If a word can be both a common and proper noun, such as **Jack** and **jack**, write it both ways.

READING & WRITING

sand	mice
stand	twice
hand	nice

RHYMES

NOVEMBER

READING & WRITING

sand	mice
stand	twice
hand	nice

RHYMES

When all of the children who think they can complete words with their beginning letters have done so, call up children to make the words which are not yet displayed by saying something like, "I think the person with the **str** card could come up here and add **str** to **and** to make a word we know."

Try to include all of the words that any of the children would have in their listening vocabulary but avoid obscure words. If all of the patterns you wrote to begin the chart are used to make complete words, add as many as needed. Finally, if you or the students can think of good longer words that rhyme and have the spelling pattern, add them to the list. (Spell and write the whole word since children do not have the extra letters needed to spell it.)

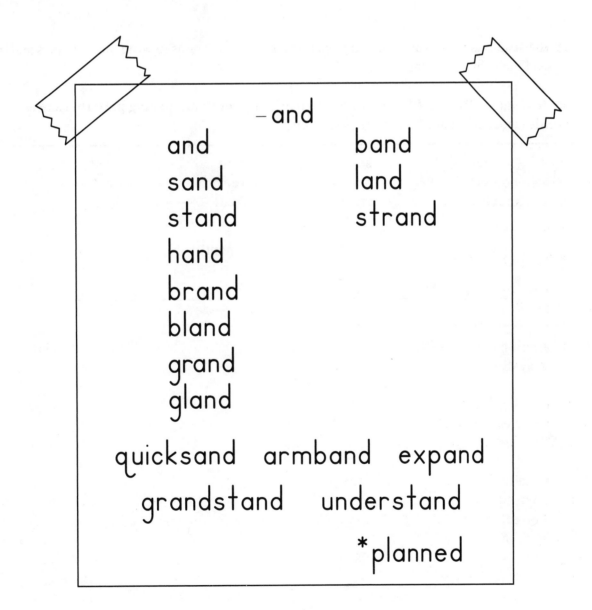

– and

and	band
sand	land
stand	strand
hand	
brand	
bland	
grand	
gland	

quicksand   armband   expand

grandstand   understand

*planned

READING & WRITING

sand | mice
stand | twice
hand | nice

RHYMES

NOVEMBER

READING & WRITING

sand | mice
stand | twice
hand | nice

RHYMES

❹ Once the chart of rhyming words is written, work together in a shared writing format to write a couple of sentences using lots of the rhyming words. After generating a list of rhyming **and** words, one class came up with the silly rhyme at right.

Around the gr<u>andst</u>and
was <u>land</u> and s<u>and</u>.
On the st<u>and</u>
was a gr<u>and</u> b<u>and</u>.

❺ **Next, the students write rhymes.** Many teachers put them in teams to write these rhymes and then let them read their rhymes to the class.

You can do *Reading/Writing Rhymes* **lessons to teach any common spelling pattern.** Here are some of the words students might use with the pattern **ent**:

ent	sent	bent	spent
cent	went	vent	dent
Kent	Brent	Trent	lent
rent	tent		
event	invent	torment	
			*meant

Making Words

20 min.

This month, there are three *Making Words* lessons related to the theme of community, which is a part of the social studies curriculum in many third grades.

The steps for each *Making Words* lesson are as follows. (See page 35 for steps in preparing for the lesson.)

1. Give students the letter strips, have them write uppercase letters on the back, and have them cut or tear the strips apart into letters. Place corresponding large letter cards along the chalk ledge or in a pocket chart.

2. Tell students which words to make. Let them know when they need to add a letter or change the order of letters. Use sentences for words when students might not immediately recognize the meaning.

3. Have one student come and make each word with the big letters. Other students should correct their words if they are not spelled correctly. Keep a brisk pace. Do not wait for everyone to make each word before sending someone up to make it with the big letters.

4. Give the students a minute to see if they can come up with the secret word. If no one can figure it out, give them clues or tell them the word and have them make it.

5. Have students sort the words into patterns. Sort first for words with the same root or ending and then for rhymes.

6. When the rhyming words are sorted, remind the students that rhyming words can help them read and spell words. Write two new rhyming words on cards and have students place these words in the correct columns and use the rhymes to decode them. Finally, say two rhyming words and help them see how the familiar words help spell them.

7. Give students a clean copy of the same letter strip and have them write the uppercase letters on the back. Let students take these strips home. Challenge them to bring in a long list of words you "weren't smart enough to think of" and ask them if they think their families will figure out the secret word.

Here are three *Making Words* lessons for this month. (The **/** indicates words that can be made by simply rearranging the same letters.)

Lesson One: **Secret Word: community**

Letters: i o u c m m n t y

Make: not, cot, cut, nut, mom, Tom, into, city, tiny, unity, mount, count, county, mutiny, **community**

Sort : words ending in **y**: city, tiny, unity, county, mutiny, community

  rhyming words: not, cot
  nut, cut
  count, mount
  mom, Tom

Transfer : prom, plot, strut, clot

Lesson Two: **Secret Word: neighbors**

Letters: e i o b g h n r s

Make: sob, rob, rose, nose, horn, born, bore, shore, snore, ignore, boring, nosier/senior, regions, **neighbors**

Sort: related words: bore, boring, nose, nosier

  rhyming words: sob, rob
  rose, nose
  horn, born
  bore, shore, snore, ignore

Transfer: score, those, throb, thorn

Lesson Three: **Secret Word: history**

Letters: i o h r s t y

Make: it, hit, hot, try, shy, toy, Roy, shot, sort, short, story, shorty, **history**

Sort: related words: short, shorty

  rhyming words: it, hit
  hot, shot
  try, shy
  toy, Roy
  sort, short

Transfer: sport, dry, slot, grit

Using Words You Know

20 min.

This month's *Using Words You Know* lessons will **review the long vowel sounds and focus student attention on how the vowel sounds change in spelling patterns that are the same except for the vowel.** All of the lessons for this goal work in a similar fashion. Here are the steps (see pages 18-20 for a sample lesson):

1. Display and talk about the words.

2. Identify the spelling patterns.

3. Make as many columns as needed on the board, chart, or transparency and on student papers. Head these with the words and underline the spelling patterns.

4. Show students one-syllable words written on index cards. Have students write each word in the column showing the same pattern and use the rhyme to pronounce it.

5. Say one-syllable words and have students decide how to spell them by deciding which word they rhyme with.

6. Repeat the above procedure with longer words.

7. Help students verbalize how words they know help them read and spell lots of other words, including longer words.

Following are two *Using Words You Know* lessons for this month.

Words you know:
late, Pete, kite, vote, cute

Words to read:
flute, white, write, date, chute, plate, quote, gate

Words to spell:
mute, mate, bite, quite, brute, spite, note, rate, state

Longer words to read:
athlete, appetite, absolute, imitate, satellite, dynamite, complete, commute, remote, translate

Longer words to spell:
parachute, polite, invite, compute, compete, delete, devote, locate, promote, donate

Using Words You Know — tan... plan

Words you know:
Jane, gene, line, bone, tune

Words to read:
phone, crane, scene, spine, throne, prune, shrine, plane

Words to spell:
cone, zone, dune, June, pine, stone, shine, sane

Longer words to read:
cyclone, hurricane, immune, postpone, Yellowstone, Neptune, headline, deadline, intervene, tombstone

Longer words to spell:
airplane, underline, headphone, backbone, sunshine, insane, microphone, Irene

---

The finished charts should look like this:

late	Pete	kite	vote	cute
date	athlete	white	quote	flute
plate	complete	write	note	chute
gate	compete	bite	remote	mute
mate	delete	quite	devote	brute
rate		spite	promote	absolute
state		appetite		commute
imitate		satellite		parachute
translate		dynamite		compute
locate		polite		
donate		invite		

Jane	gene	line	bone	tune
crane	scene	spine	phone	prune
plane	intervene	shrine	throne	dune
sane	Irene	pine	cone	June
hurricane		shine	zone	immune
airplane		headline	stone	Neptune
insane		deadline	cyclone	
		underline	postpone	
		sunshine	Yellowstone	
			tombstone	
			headphone	
			backbone	
			microphone	

Guess the covered **word.**

Guess the covered **word.**

Guess the Covered Word

20 min.

Remember to provide practice with cross checking by occasionally giving students some sentences or a paragraph in which they must guess some words, first with no letters showing and then with all of the letters up to the vowel showing. Students should become good at using meaning, beginning letters, and word length to figure out words. Try using paragraphs related to science or social studies units for cross checking practice. This allows you to review or introduce content information. You can also stress the notion that students should use the same strategies when reading in the subject areas as they do during "reading." Here is an example related to the social studies topic of communities. Of course, you may adapt this to your community!

Communities

All over the | world |, people live in communities. Some of these communities are small | villages |. Other communities are | huge | cities. There are differences among communities but there are also | many | similarities. All communities have some stores and | businesses |. Communities have | churches | and schools. They have | places | where people work. Communities have | governments |. Sometimes, a community has a town | council | or a board of | commissioners |. Most communities have a | mayor | and a town or city manager.

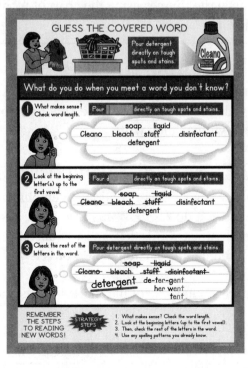

*Chart shown is from Carson-Dellosa's *Word Wall "Plus" for Third Grade* (CD-2504).

Making These Activities Multilevel

How *Reading/Writing Rhymes* Is Multilevel

This month's new activity, *Reading/Writing Rhymes* is multilevel in much the same way that *Using Words You Know* and *Making Words* are:

- The oral concept of rhyme and the idea that words which rhyme usually have the same spelling pattern are reviewed in each lesson.

- All of the beginning letters (onsets) are reviewed and, if students need lots of practice with these, you can have them say the sound for each onset as you hand out the cards. If you have some children still struggling with the simplest beginning sounds, give them the single consonant cards and give the more complex onset cards to your more sophisticated readers.

- Adding some common words with different spelling patterns to your list helps your students develop a "set for diversity" and reminds them that, when dealing with English spelling patterns, they should think "usually" and "almost always."

- Adding a few big words at the end allows students to write more interesting rhymes and helps your accelerated readers become automatic at noticing patterns they know at the ends of longer words.

- Of course, as your students write rhymes using the chart of words, they write on a variety of levels, but they all enjoy it.

How the *Word Wall* Is Multilevel

The addition of more homophones and using *Word Wall* words to spell other words should help your *Word Wall* meet the needs of a wide range of children. Be sure that you remind them about spelling *Word Wall* words correctly in "everything" they write.

How *Using Words You Know* and *Making Words* Are Multilevel

If you have many struggling readers in your class, continue to emphasize stretching words out to hear all of the letters up to the vowel as you do *Using Words You Know* and *Making Words*. Also remind students how to use patterns from rhyming words they know to decode and spell other words. Remember that the transfer to actually decoding and spelling new words is what you are seeking.

If you have mostly advanced readers, skip some of the shorter words and emphasize the longer words in these lessons.

Applying Strategies When Reading and Writing

Keep reminding your kids that they are "third graders now" and they are becoming more independent and responsible—more grown up! Help them see that some of the things you are doing with words are moving them toward that goal. They should be able to tell you that in addition to "pesky" illogical words and examples to help remember spelling changes needed when adding endings, the *Word Wall* now has **-ful, -less, dis-,** and **re-** words which help decode and spell similar words.

As students prepare to read, ask them what they will do when they come to unfamiliar words. Have them explain in their own words how they will use patterns and cross checking. Remind them to always check their pronunciation to make sure it makes sense and "sounds right."

When you are reading with a small group or individual children, coach them to use their strategies instead of telling them the words. Here are some suggestions for encouraging students to use their new strategies:

1. When a child comes to an unknown word and looks up at you, say, "Put your finger on the word and say all of the letters."

2. If the child correctly pronounces the word after saying all of the letters, let that child know what she did that worked by saying something like, "Terrific. That's what good readers do. They meet lot of words they don't immediately recognize but they look at all the letters and can often figure them out."

3. If the child does not correctly pronounce the word after saying all of the letters, say, "Keep your finger there so you can get right back to that word, then finish the sentence."

4. If the child correctly pronounces the word, point out the strategy used, "See. You didn't know the word but when you finished the sentence and thought about what would make sense and begin with all of the right letters and was about the right length you could figure it out."

5. If the child cannot figure it out after reading the sentence, give a pattern clue: "Let's see, the word is spelled **r-e-s-i-s-t**. You know **re-** from **recycle**. Do you know an **ist** word like **list** or **fist** that would help you with the last chunk?"

6. You may also point out a picture clue, "That's a hard word to figure out, but you can tell by looking at the picture that a really bad storm is coming. Think about what we might call a storm like the one you see in the picture. It begins with **tr** and ends in **ous**. That's right, 'a **treacherous** storm.' Sometimes, the picture can help us with unusual words."

If you will persevere in "coaching" instead of "doing it for them," even your most recalcitrant third graders will begin to use what they are learning when they need it.

Month at a Glance

December is one of those months when it is hard to get even the "routine" things done. There is no new activity for this shortened, hectic school month.

Here is what will be suggested for December:
- expanding the *Word Wall* by adding 14 more words, including compound words, contractions, and words with the suffix **-en**
- *Using Words You Know* lessons that review vowel sounds when the vowel is followed by **r**
- *Guess the Covered Word* in paragraph form, focused on holidays
- *Making Words* lessons related to the holidays
- *Reading/Writing Rhymes* for pattern decoding and spelling using the **ine** and **out** patterns

Here are some time guidelines to consider this month:

Class with Most Children On Grade Level
- 5 minutes *Word Wall* practice daily
- Three 20-minute word lessons each week, including *Reading/Writing Rhymes, Using Words You Know, Making Words,* and *Guess the Covered Word*

Class with Most Children Struggling with Grade-Level Material
- 10 minutes *Word Wall* practice daily
- One 20-minute word lesson every day, including *Reading/Writing Rhymes, Using Words You Know, Making Words,* and *Guess the Covered Word*

Class with Almost All Children On or Above Grade Level
- 5 minutes *Word Wall* practice daily
- Two 20-minute word lessons each week, picking and choosing from *Reading/Writing Rhymes, Using Words You Know, Making Words,* and *Guess the Covered Word*

Word Wall

10 min.

Words for this month include some commonly misspelled words, contractions, homophones, compound words, an example for the **en** suffix, and another example of consonant doubling:

anyone	**are**	**can't**	**don't**	**everybody**	**everything**	**hidden**
our	**right**	**terrible**	**trouble**	**won't**	**wouldn't**	**write**

❶ Add the words to your display. When adding words that begin with the same letter, use different colors. Use different colors for **write** and **right**. Attach a pencil to the word **write** to help students differentiate it from **right**. If you are also using the portable *Word Walls*, give students a new sheet to which the new words (and clues) have been added (see page 157 for a reproducible).

❷ Focus student attention on each word and have students chant it, cheerleader-style. Before cheering for each word, help students notice patterns and point out "illogicalities" as needed:

are	Other words that end in **are** rhyme with **care** and **spare**.
anyone, everybody, everything	These are examples of compound words with **any** and **every**.
can't, don't, won't, wouldn't	These are contractions for **cannot**, **do not**, **will not**, and **would not**. Don't forget the clicking gesture and sound. Remind students that **would** is spelled like **could**.
hidden	Something that you **hid** is **hidden**. Other words in which the **en** works like this include **written** and **frozen**. Help students notice that the **d** is doubled just like the **t** in **getting**.
our	**Our** is spelled logically like **sour** and **flour**; in some parts of the country it is pronounced like **are**. If **our** and **are** are homophones in the dialect of your students, add a clue such as "Our Class" to **our**.
right/write	Students will not need to have the pencil or its function pointed out. Explain that there are other words, such as **wreck** and **wrestling**, which begin with **wr**.
terrible	This is often misspelled with only one **r** or with an **el** at the end.
trouble	This has an illogical spelling but the same pattern used in the word **double**. Have students notice that **people**, **recycle**, **terrible**, and **trouble** all end with the **le** pattern.

3 Use writing clues to have students write each word. Make sure that clues distinguish these words from each other and from last month's words. Here are some possibilities:

Word Wall Riddles

1. Number 1 is the compound word that ends in **thing**.

2. Number 2 is the compound word that begins with **any**.

3. For number 3, write the contraction that means **cannot**.

4. For number 4, write the contraction that means **do not**.

5. For number 5, write the contraction that means **would not**.

6. For number 6, write the five-letter word you need a pencil to do.

7. For number 7, write the other word that is pronounced just like the word you wrote for 6.

Answer Key: 1. **everything** 2. **anyone** 3. **can't** 4. **don't** 5. **wouldn't** 6. **write** 7. **right**

After the students write the words, have them check their own papers by once more chanting the letters aloud, underlining each letter as they say it.

4 Continue to practice words from the complete list using cheering and writing modes. Be diligent in writing "WW" next to any *Word Wall* word misspelled on anything!

Extending the *Word Wall* to Other Words

Students now have 56 words on the wall—more than half the words they will be expected to learn this year. They should also be able to spell lots of other words, including these from previous months:

---

should	would	cause	cities	communities	country
excite	excited	get	laugh	laughing	school
beauty	cover	covers	covered	covering	recover
recovers	recovered	recovering	discovers	discovered	discovering
rough	tough	hope	hopes	hoped	hoping
		hopeful			

In addition, students should now be able to spell the following:

---

shouldn't   couldn't   anything   everyone   hiding   troubling   writing   written

---

Show them how the new suffix **-en** can help them spell other words:

If you can spell **bite**, **take**, and **forgot**, how would you spell **bitten**, **taken**, and **forgotten**?

You probably won't have time in this busy and short month, but if you do, you could have a contest and make a banner with the suffix **-en** (see page 34 for directions).

Reading/Writing Rhymes

This month's *Reading/Writing Rhymes* lessons use the **ine** and **out** patterns. The steps for a *Reading/Writing Rhymes* lesson are as follows (see pages 52-54 for steps in preparing a lesson):

1. Distribute the onset deck to the students. If initial letter sounds still need practice, have students say the sound for each onset as you distribute it.

2. Once all of the onset cards are distributed, write the spelling pattern with which you are working 10-12 times on a piece of chart paper. As you write it each time, have the children help spell it and pronounce it.

3. Invite each child who has a card that he thinks makes a word to come to the front of the class, place the card next to one of the written spelling patterns, and pronounce the word. If the word is indeed real , use the word in a sentence and write it on the chart. If the word is not real, explain why you cannot write it on the chart. If a word is real and does rhyme but has a different spelling pattern, such as **planned** to rhyme with **and**, explain that it rhymes but has a different pattern, and include it at the bottom of the chart with an asterisk next to it. Write names with uppercase initial letters and, if a word can be both a common and proper noun, such as **jack** and **Jack**, write it both ways.

4. When all of the children who think they can spell words with their beginning letters and the spelling pattern have done so, call children up to make other words by saying something like, "I think the person with the **br** card could come up here and add **br** to **ine** to make a word we know." If the patterns you wrote to begin the chart are all made into complete words, add as many more as needed.

5. If you can think of some longer words that rhyme and have the spelling pattern, add them to the list. Spell and write the longer words since children do not have the extra letters needed to spell them.

6. Once the chart of rhyming words is written, work together in a shared writing format to write a couple of sentences using lots of the rhyming words.

7. Give student a few minutes to work individually or with friends to write some silly text using as many rhyming words as they can.

Here are some words you might include on the charts this month:

ine	
fine	dine
mine	line
nine	shine
whine	vine
spine	pine
brine	wine
twine	swine
airline	headline
valentine	porcupine
*sign, Frankenstein®	

out	
out	shout
stout	spout
snout	trout
pout	clout
scout	sprout
bout	rout
without	cookout
workout	about
*drought, doubt	

Making Words

20 min.

This month, we have three *Making Words* lessons related to the holidays. (The / indicates words that can be made by simply rearranging the same letters.)

Lesson One:	**Secret Word: Christmas**
Letters on strip:	a i c h m r s s t
Make:	arm, art, air, hair, harm, mash, cash, cart, chart, charm, chair, smart, smash, trash, Christmas
Sort for: rhyming words:	arm, harm, charm; art, cart, chart, smart air, hair, chair; mash, cash, smash, trash
Transfer Words:	affair, alarm, apart, clash

Lesson Two:	**Secret Word: traditions**
Letters on strip:	a i i o d n r s t t
Make:	art, dart, dirt, toad, road, roast, toast, radio, drain, train, strain, strand, artist, station, traditions
Sort for: related words:	art, artist
words ending in **-tion**:	traditions, station
rhyming words:	art, dart; toad, road; toast, roast; drain, train, strain
Transfer Words:	unload, restart, remain, boast

Lesson Three:	**Secret Word: decorate**
Letters on strip:	a e e o c d r t
Make:	act, care, dare/dear, deer, date, rate, race, actor, trace/react/crate, create, created, decorate
Sort for: related words:	act, react, actor; create, created
homophones:	dear, deer
rhyming words:	care, dare; date, rate, crate, create, decorate race, trace
Transfer Words:	replace, aware, rebate, unlace

Using Words You Know

20 min.

This month's *Using Words You Know* lessons review the vowel sounds when the vowel is followed by **r**. The steps are as follows (see pages 18-20 for a sample lesson):

1. Display and talk about the words.

2. Identify the spelling patterns.

3. Make as many columns as needed on the board, chart, or transparency and on student papers. Head these with the words and underline the spelling patterns.

4. Show students one-syllable words written on index cards. Have them write each word in the column with the same pattern and use the rhyme to pronounce it.

5. Say one-syllable words and have students decide how to spell them by deciding with which column each rhymes.

6. Repeat the above procedure with longer words.

7. Help students verbalize how words they know help them read and spell lots of other words, including longer words.

Here are two *Using Words You Know* lessons for this month:

Words you know:
a<u>rt</u>, j<u>erk</u>, d<u>irt</u>, sp<u>ort</u>, b<u>urn</u>

Words to read:
churn, chart, port, fort, flirt, skirt, part, clerk

Words to spell:
perk, shirt, sort, snort, turn, short, smart, start, squirt

Longer words to read:
transport, depart, nightshirt, support, berserk, heartburn, restart, passport

Longer words to spell:
apart, airport, sunburn, redshirt, outsmart, report, export, import

Words you know:
d<u>ar</u>k, h<u>er</u>, g<u>ir</u>l, h<u>or</u>n, h<u>ur</u>t

Words to read:
bark, spurt, corn, thorn, Kurt, spark, whirl, Clark, per

Words to spell:
born, blurt, swirl, mark, sworn, torn, twirl, shark

Longer words to read:
birthmark, shoehorn, yogurt, newborn, Denmark, offer, aardvark, prefer

Longer words to spell:
foghorn, trademark, unhurt, unicorn, ballpark, popcorn, remark, refer

Finished charts should look like this:

<u>ar</u>t	j<u>er</u>k	d<u>ir</u>t	sp<u>or</u>t	b<u>ur</u>n
chart	clerk	skirt	port	churn
part	perk	flirt	fort	turn
smart	berserk	shirt	sort	heartburn
start		squirt	snort	sunburn
depart		nightshirt	short	
restart		redshirt	transport	
apart			support	
outsmart			passport	
			airport	
			report	
			export	
			import	

d<u>ar</u>k	h<u>er</u>	g<u>ir</u>l	h<u>or</u>n	h<u>ur</u>t
bark	per	whirl	corn	spurt
spark	offer	swirl	thorn	Kurt
Clark	prefer	twirl	born	blurt
mark	refer		sworn	yogurt
shark			torn	unhurt
birthmark			shoehorn	
Denmark			newborn	
aardvark			foghorn	
trademark			unicorn	
ballpark			popcorn	
remark				

Guess the covered word.

Guess the covered word.

Guess the Covered Word

20 min.

The holidays are a focus of interest for everyone. Consider doing a *Guess the Covered Word* lesson using a paragraph about how different people celebrate the holidays, or some of the things you and your children might do over the long holiday break:

Winter Holidays

The winter holidays are a fun time for everyone. Some people take trips to visit relatives who live in distant states. Some people even go to other countries over the long winter break. Families usually get together and have festive meals. The older relatives tell stories about the holidays when they were young. Many people like to watch or go to sports events during the holidays. Other people like to do the sports instead of just watching. In cold places, like Colorado, people skate, ski, and go bobsledding. In warm places, like Florida, people swim, surf, and go scuba diving. After a good relaxing winter break, we should all be eager to get back to school!

 # Making These Activities Multilevel

How the *Word Wall* Is Multilevel

The addition of more homophones, and using *Word Wall* words to spell other words, should help your *Word Wall* meet the needs of a wide range of children. Be sure that you remind them about spelling *Word Wall* words correctly in everything they write. Emphasize other words that the *Word Wall* words will help them spell.

How the Other Activities Are Multilevel

If you have many struggling readers in your class, continue to emphasize the technique of stretching out words to hear onsets as you do *Reading/Writing Rhymes, Using Words You Know,* and *Making Words* lessons. **Remind students how to use patterns from rhyming words they know to decode and spell other words. Remember that the transfer to actually decoding and spelling new words is what you are seeking.**

If you have mostly advanced readers, skip some of the shorter words and emphasize the longer words in these lessons.

Applying Strategies When Reading and Writing

Your students should be using what they know as they read and write. If they forget, ask them what they should do instead of telling them:

When a child is reading with you, comes to an unknown word, and looks up at you with a blank stare, say, "What do you do when you come to a word you don't immediately recognize."

If the child responds, "Put my finger on the word and say all of the letters," smile and say, "See—you do know what to do!"

If the child claims not to know, tell him or let another child in the group tell him (what to do— not the unknown word!) and lead him once again through the procedures of reading to the end of the sentence and then using context, patterns, and picture clues as appropriate.

When you are editing with a child on a piece she is going to publish, ask questions:

- "Where in the room can you find the word **they're** with a clue next to it so that you can figure out on your own which one you need in this sentence?"

- "You spelled **crate c-r-a-t**. You know lots of **at** words and they don't rhyme with **crate**. What words do you know that rhyme with **crate** and could help you with the pattern?"

Remember that phonics and spelling knowledge are only useful if your students actually use them when they need them. Continue to teach good multilevel lessons and then "nag" students a little when they need it.

Month at a Glance

A new month and a new year! Did you make any resolutions? What about your students? Do they need to be reminded that they are halfway through third grade and will soon be really grown-up fourth graders? Do you and they need to reaffirm your resolve for independence and responsibility? This month, a new activity will be introduced which is just perfect for the second half of third grade: *Word Sorts and Hunts*. This chapter will help you remind your students how word activities help them become independent, sophisticated readers and writers.

This month, the following will be suggested:

- reviewing *Word Wall* words and expanding the *Word Wall* by adding 14 more words, including the homophones **knew/new** and **know/no**, and words with the suffix **-ly**
- playing *Be a Mind Reader*, a game to reinforce knowledge of the *Word Wall* words
- *Using Words You Know* has students verbalize how the strategy helps them. This month's lessons focus on the **ll** and **ss** final spelling patterns.
- *Guess the Covered Word* focuses on word length awareness with a paragraph including covered words that are unusually short and long.
- *Making Words* lessons focus on students being able to verbalize how the make, sort, and transfer steps help them to be better readers and writers.
- *Reading/Writing Rhymes* for the rest of the year will focus on rhymes with two common spelling patterns and the development of the "looks right" strategy. This month's patterns are **ain/ane** and **ait/ate**.
- introducing *Word Sorts and Hunts* with **u**, **ue**, **u–e**, **ur**, **sure**, and **ture**

Here are some time guidelines to consider this month:

Class with Most Children On Grade Level

- 5 minutes *Word Wall* practice daily
- Three 20-minute word lessons each week, including *Word Sorts and Hunts, Reading/Writing Rhymes, Using Words You Know, Making Words,* and *Guess the Covered Word*

Class with Most Children Struggling with Grade-Level Material

- 10 minutes *Word Wall* practice daily
- One 20-minute word lesson every day, including *Word Sorts and Hunts, Reading/Writing Rhymes, Using Words You Know, Making Words,* and *Guess the Covered Word*

Class with Almost All Children On or Above Grade Level

- 5 minutes *Word Wall* practice daily
- Two 20-minute word lessons each week, picking and choosing from *Word Sorts and Hunts, Reading/Writing Rhymes, Using Words You Know, Making Words,* and *Guess the Covered Word*

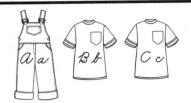

Word Wall

10 min.

Before adding this month's new words, review with students how the *Word Wall* helps them write like grown-ups instead of children. Ask them questions about the "illogical" words and get them to talk about how the brain makes something automatic after it is done a number of times. Remind them that they have to practice the correct spellings of these "illogical" words often in order to get the old, logical but incorrect, spellings replaced with the correct spellings. Let each student identify five of these illogical words that are most troublesome for him and make a reminder list to display on his desk.

Next, talk about the words that are on the *Word Wall* so that students recognize examples of spelling changes and common prefixes and suffixes. Help students see that they should use these words whenever they are trying to spell similar words. These words are examples for the patterns. Good spellers don't study every word; they learn the patterns and then notice which words follow the patterns. Challenge your students—especially your quick word learners—to use the spelling change and prefix/suffix examples to spell similar words correctly in all their writing.

Finally, **identify the compound words, contractions, and homophones**. Remind students how the clues next to all but one of the homophones help them know which one they are writing. **Tell them that many people find it easier to remember where to put the apostrophe in a contraction by chanting the spelling of the contraction and putting a "click" where the apostrophe was.** Remind them of the other compounds and contractions that are similar to the ones on the wall and challenge them to try to spell these correctly in their writing too.

Once you have duly reminded your students that the *Word Wall* is only useful if they make maximum use of it in their writing, add this month's new words. See if your students can tell you why these words were chosen to be third-grade *Word Wall* words. This month's words include some commonly misspelled words, some homophones, and words with the suffix **-ly**.

about	especially	except	friendly	knew	new	know
no	myself	really	probably	then	usually	what

❶ **Add the words to your display.** When adding words that begin with the same letter, use different colors. Use different colors for **knew**, **new**, **know**, and **no**. Attach cards saying "old" and "yes" to **new** and **no**. If you are also using the portable *Word Walls*, give students a new sheet to which the new words (and clues) have been added (see page 158 for a reproducible).

❷ **Focus student attention on each word and have students chant it, cheerleader-style. Before cheering for each word, point out anything illogical about the word and discuss common patterns:**

about	This is another word like **again** in which the beginning syllable is spelled with an **a**.
especially	Point out the word **special** and the ending **-ly**.
except	This starts with **ex-** like **excited** and then rhymes with and is spelled like **kept** and **slept**.
friendly	Here is the word **friend** with the suffix **-ly**. The tricky part about **friend** is the unexplainable **i**.
knew/new, **know/no**	Here are more words pronounced the same but with different meanings. A few other words in English, such as **knock**, **knee**, and **knuckle**, begin with **kn**.
myself	This is a compound word with **my** and **self**. Other **self** compounds include **yourself** and **himself**.
probably	This is another word that ends in **-ly**. Often misspelled because it is commonly pronounced "probly."
really	**Really** is the word **real** with the suffix **-ly**.
then	This is spelled logically but often misspelled as **thin** or **than**, particularly if pronounced like those words. **Then** rhymes with and has the same spelling pattern as **when**.
usually	Here is **usual** with **-ly** added at end, like **really**.
what	Other words spelled like this rhyme with **at**, **cat**, and **that**.

❸ Use writing clues to have students write each word. Make sure that the clues distinguish these words from each other and from last month's words. Here are some possibilities:

Word Wall Riddles

1. Number 1 is a five-letter word that starts with **a** and ends with **t**.

2. Number 2 is the four-letter word that starts with **wh** and ends with **t**.

3. For number 3, write the opposite of **yes**.

4. For number 4, write the other word that is pronounced just like the word you wrote for 3.

5. For number 5, write the opposite of **old**.

6. For number 6, write the other word that is pronounced just like the word you wrote for 5.

7. For number 7, write the seven-letter word that ends in **-ly**.

Answer Key: 1. **about** 2. **what** 3. **no** 4. **know** 5. **new** 6. **knew** 7. **usually**

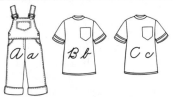

After students write the words, have them check their own papers by once more chanting the letters aloud, underlining each letter as they say it.

❹ Continue to practice words by cheering and writing when you have time and hold students accountable in their writing for all *Word Wall* words. If you have been resolute, you should be seeing consistent improvement in the spelling of these high-frequency words in student writing.

Extending the *Word Wall* to Other Words

Students now have 70 words they are spelling automatically and fluently. They should also be able to spell lots of other words, including these from previous months:

should	would	cause	cities	communities	country	excite
excited	get	laugh	laughing	school	beauty	cover
covers	covered	covering	recover	recovers	recovered	recovering
discovers	discovered	discovering	rough	tough	hope	hopes
hoped	hoping	hopeful	shouldn't	couldn't	anything	everyone
	hiding	troubling		writing	written	

In addition, they should now be able to spell these words:

special	friend	friendlier	friendliest	newer
newest	real	usual	excitedly	beautifully
	hopelessly	hopefully	terribly	

Show them how the new suffix **-ly** can help them spell other words:

If you can spell **rich**, **happy**, and **nice**, how would you spell **richly**, **happily**, and **nicely**?

If your students enjoy the contests and banner, consider doing one with the suffix **-ly** (see page 34 for directions).

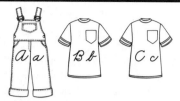 

Reviewing with *Be a Mind Reader*

Now that you have 70 words on the wall, you have enough to play one of students' favorite games and give them practice with the words at the same time. **In *Be a Mind Reader*, you think of a word and give students five clues which narrow to only one possible word.** Everyone should get it by the last clue, but did anyone "read your mind" and get it on an earlier clue? Have students number from 1 to 5 and give five clues such as these:

---

1. It's one of our *Word Wall* words. (Students hate this but often someone guesses it and then they love it! You can narrow this a little if you like by saying, "It's one of our *Word Wall* words in the first half of the alphabet—between **a** and **m**." Have them write their guess next to number 1.)

2. It has four letters. (This narrows it down considerably! If they have a four-letter word for number 1, they should write it again. If not, they need to choose and write one with four letters.)

3. It does not begin with a **w**. (This eliminates **want**, **went**, **when**, **won't**, and **what**.)

4. It does not have any **a**'s (There are six choices left: **into**, **very**, **city**, **don't**, **knew**, and **know**.)

5. It fits in this sentence: I want to go to New York _____!

Answer: city

By now, everyone should have it, but find out who had it on any of the earlier clues and express amazement that they read your mind! Here's another example:

---

1. It's one of our *Word Wall* words.

2. It has six or more letters.

3. It ends in **-ly**.

4. It does not have an **e** in it.

5. It has the word **usual** in it.

Answer: **usually**

Kids love *Be a Mind Reader*, and it gives them lots of "painless" practice.

Word Sorts and Hunts

Word Sorts (Henderson, 1990) **have long been advocated as an activity to help children develop the habit of analyzing words to look for patterns.** There are a variety of ways to do *Word Sorts*, but the basic principles are the same. Children look at words and sort them into categories based on spelling patterns and sound. Children say the words and look at how they are spelled. They learn that, to go in the same category, the words must "sound the same and look the same."

It is important that children develop speed and accuracy as they sort. **Many teachers begin by showing the children the words, then having the children say the words and put them in the appropriate categories.**

When the children are proficient at looking, saying, and deciding, the teacher leads them in some "blind sorting." The teacher calls out the same words but does not show them to the children. Children decide in which column each word should be written before the word is shown. The children indicate where they think the word should go by pointing to the column, the teacher shows them the word to confirm, and the word is written in the correct column.

The final stage in developing automatic spelling of certain patterns is the "blind writing sort." The teacher calls out some of the previously sorted words and children write them in the appropriate columns before seeing them. Once the children have written the word, the teacher shows the word so that they may confirm their spelling and categorization.

Word Sorts **are followed by** *Word Hunts*. For these, many teachers post charts with the categories the class has studied. Children are encouraged to add words that fit the patterns any time they find them in their reading. Some children keep word notebooks and add words they find that fit particular categories. **Hunting for words is a critical transfer step because it draws children's attention to spelling patterns in the "real" materials they are reading.**

The last half of third grade is a good time to use *Word Sorts and Hunts* to review all of the common sounds and spellings for vowel patterns. For the first lessons, the vowel u is used because it has the least number of common patterns. In the next four months, *Word Sorts and Hunts* for the other four vowels will be outlined. For each vowel, spend a week sorting and a week hunting.

Sorting Words with *U*

❶ Use the reproducible sheets on pages 170-174 to make a transparency for yourself and sorting sheets for the students, or create your own. On the first day, each child has a sort sheet and the teacher has a transparency that looks like this:

Other	**u**	**ue**	**u–e**	**u–e**	**ur**	**sure**	**ture**
judge	us	blue	use	tune	burn	insure	nature

❷ Have your students fold their sheets so that they can't see the last two columns (**sure** and **ture**). Cover those two columns on your transparency. Have the children pronounce each of the key words and notice the spelling pattern.

❸ Explain that you are going to show words to the class and they must decide in which column each word fits. **To go in a column, the word must have the same spelling pattern and the same sound.** Help them see that the word **judge** has the **u–e** pattern but cannot go in that column because it does not have the same sound you hear in **use** or **tune**. **The "other" column is where students will put the tricky words—the ones that don't follow the logical patterns.** To decide where to put each word, students **must look at the letters and listen to the sound**. Challenge them to not let you "trick them" with some of your tricky words!

❹ Show children 15-20 words which have the vowel **u**. As you show each word, have students pronounce the word and then write it in the column in which they think it belongs. Choose a child to come write the word in the correct column on your transparency, then continue with the next word. At the end of the first day, your transparency and their sort sheets might look like this:

Other	**u**	**ue**	**u–e**	**u–e**	**ur**
judge	us	blue	use	tune	burn
suit	run	true	mule	dune	turn
touch	must	sue	mute	rude	burp
	club	due	cute		
	hunt		cure		

5 On the second day, use the same sheet and keep the last two columns covered. Show another 15-20 words and have students sort them into the first six columns. Include some words with more than one syllable and help children focus on the syllable that has the **u** in it. Be sure to have students pronounce each word before writing it and remind them to watch for tricky words. They can't just look at the letters, but must also listen for the sounds.

Other	**u**	**ue**	**u–e**	**u–e**	**ur**
judge	**us**	**blue**	**use**	**tune**	**burn**
suit	run	true	mule	dune	turn
touch	must	sue	mute	rude	burp
tuna	club	due	cute	flute	turtle
bruise	hunt	glue	cure	salute	urban
menu	drum	pursue	amuse	dude	fur
	bus	clue	dispute		

6 On the third day, use all the columns. Show students another 15-20 words and have them pronounce and then write them in the appropriate columns. This is what the sheets might look like at the end of the third day:

Other	**u**	**ue**	**u–e**	**u–e**	**ur**	**sure**	**ture**
judge	**us**	**blue**	**use**	**tune**	**burn**	**insure**	**nature**
suit	run	true	mule	dune	turn	measure	creature
touch	must	sue	mute	rude	burp	assure	picture
tuna	club	due	cute	flute	turtle	treasure	mixture
bruise	hunt	glue	cure	salute	urban	pleasure	mature
menu	drum	pursue	amuse	dude	fur		adventure
cruise	bus	clue	dispute	pollute	return		
fudge	number	statue	compute				
	minus	avenue					

7 The first three days of sorting were all "reading sorts." The students looked at and pronounced each word before deciding in which column it belonged. On the fourth day, do a "blind sort." Give the children a new sorting sheet just like the one they used the first three days and use a new transparency. Pick 15-20 words already sorted but say each word without showing it. Have the children indicate where they think it belongs by putting a finger on the column. When the children are pointing at the column, show them the word and have them write it where it belongs.

❽ The final activity for the fifth day is a "blind writing sort." Again, choose 15-20 words already sorted on days 1-3 but, instead of showing the word, say the word and have students try to write it in the correct column before you show them the word. Depending on the level of your class, you may want to use some of the easier words on this fifth day. If you use some of the more sophisticated words, praise students for writing them in the correct columns even if the words are not spelled completely correctly. Have students correct any incorrect letters after someone writes the word on the transparency. By the end of the fifth day, all of your students should have a much better notion of some of the common spelling patterns for the vowel **u**.

Word Hunts

Next week, move the children from word sorting to word hunting:

❶ Give students another clean sheet with the same columns used in the sorting activity. Tell them that they have one week to find other words that fit the patterns and write them on their sheets. Encourage students to hunt for words everywhere—around the room; on signs; in books they are reading; and while reading in science, social studies, and math. Have them keep their lists secret and encourage them to gather as many words as possible—especially big words—to contribute to the final sort.

❷ For the final sort, attach a large piece of butcher paper across the chalkboard. Set up columns just as they were on the original sort sheets, using a different color permanent marker for each. Let children take turns coming to the front of the class and writing one word in its correct column, pronouncing that word, and, for an obscure word, using it in a sentence. Words can be added until the children run out of words or until there is no more room in a particular column. If possible, hang the butcher paper somewhere in the room and encourage your students to continue to look for words for any columns that still have room.

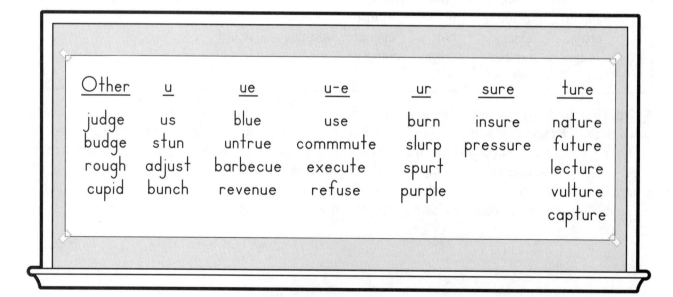

Other	u	ue	u-e	ur	sure	ture
judge	us	blue	use	burn	insure	nature
budge	stun	untrue	commmute	slurp	pressure	future
rough	adjust	barbecue	execute	spurt		lecture
cupid	bunch	revenue	refuse	purple		vulture
						capture

Reading/Writing Rhymes

20 min.

Before beginning the *Reading/Writing Rhymes* lessons this month, ask students how they use what they learn in *Reading/Writing Rhymes* when they are reading and writing. Have them explain that when they come to a word they don't immediately recognize while reading, they can often figure it out by thinking of a rhyming word they do know. **These rhyming words they know also help them with the last part of many longer words.** Have them explain also that good spellers spell by patterns, and that rhyming words often have the same spelling pattern.

Next, explain that **many rhyming words can be spelled with two common patterns**. The fact that there are two common patterns is not a problem when reading. Students quickly learn that both **ai** and **a–e** have the same sound. **When spelling a word, however, there is no way to know which one is the correct spelling unless the writer recognizes it as a word he knows after writing it.** This is why we often write a word, think, "That doesn't look right," and then try writing it with another pattern to see if that looks right.

The *Reading/Writing Rhymes* lessons for the rest of the year will help students notice the two common spelling patterns for rhymes and begin to develop their visual checking sense, which lets them know which pattern to use. When working with rhymes which have two common spelling patterns, write both patterns on the same chart. Each student comes up and tells the word his beginning letters will make, and the teacher writes it with the correct pattern. In many cases, there are homophones—words that are spelled differently and have different meanings but the same pronunciation. Write both of these and talk about what each one means.

READING & WRITING

sand	mice
stand	twice
hand	nice

RHYMES

JANUARY

READING & WRITING

sand	mice
stand	twice
hand	nice

RHYMES

The steps for a *Reading/Writing Rhymes* lesson are as follows (see pages 52-54 for preparation steps):

Here are some words for the **ain/ane** and **ait/ate** long vowel spelling patterns:

ain	ane
rain	cane
brain	crane
train	sane
pain	pane
main	mane
plain	plane
chain	Jane
drain	lane
gain	vane
grain	Shane
Spain	
stain	
strain	
vain	
sprain	

remain, explain, entertain, scatterbrain, humane, inhumane, airplane, insane, hurricane

*vein, Maine, rein, reign

ait	ate
bait	ate
wait	date
gait	gate
strait	mate
	crate
	grate
	hate
	late
	Kate
	skate
	state
	plate
	rate
	slate

classmate, migrate, candidate, irritate, graduate

*straight, eight, great, freight, weight

Making Words

20 min.

Before making words this month, see if students can tell you how *Making Words* helps they when they are reading and writing. **They should realize that they are learning how to spell many words and, more importantly, they are learning to sort words into patterns.** If they sort the new words they find into patterns as they put them in the word stores in their heads, they will have lots of words readily available to help them read and spell new words.

This month, there are three *Making Words* lessons in which the secret word is something healthy to eat. The steps for each *Making Words* lesson are as follows:

1. Give students the letter strips, have them write uppercase letters on the back, and let them cut or tear the letters apart. Place corresponding large letter cards along the chalk ledge or in a pocket chart.

2. Tell students which words to make. Let them know when they need to add a letter or change the order of letters. Use sentences for words when students might not immediately recognize the meanings.

3. Have one student come and make each word with the big letters. Other students should correct their words if they are not spelled correctly. Keep a brisk pace. Do not wait for everyone to make each word before sending someone up to make it with the big letters.

4. Give the students a minute to see if they can come up with the secret word. If no one can figure it out, give them clues or tell them the word, then have them make it.

5. Have students sort the words into patterns. Sort first for words with the same root or ending and then for rhymes.

6. When the rhyming words are sorted, remind the students that rhyming words can help them read and spell words. Write two new rhyming words on cards, and have students place these words in the correct columns and use the rhymes to decode them. Finally, say two rhyming words and help them see how the rhyming words help spell them.

7. Give students clean copies of the same letter strip and have them write the uppercase letters on the back. Send the strips home with students. Challenge them to bring in a long list of words "you weren't smart enough to think of" and ask them if they think their families will figure out the secret word.

Here are three *Making Words* lessons for January. (The / indicates words that can be made by simply rearranging the same letters.)

Lesson One:	**Secret Word: oatmeal**
Letters on strip:	a a e o l m t
Make:	at, eat/ate, mate/meat/team/tame, lame/meal, teal/late, motel, metal, tamale, oatmeal
Sort for: rhyming words:	ate, mate, late eat, meat tame, lame teal, meal, oatmeal
Transfer Words:	locate, defeat, became, ideal

Lesson Two:	**Secret Word: broccoli**
Letters on strip:	i o o b c c l r
Make:	boo, coo, cob, lob, rob, rib, oil, boil, coil, cool, crib, color, colic, broil, broccoli
Sort for: rhyming words:	oil, boil, coil, broil boo, coo rob, cob, lob rib, crib
Transfer Words:	shampoo, recoil, slob, spoil

Lesson Three:	**Secret Word: pineapples**
Letters on strip:	a e e i l n p p p s
Make:	pin, pain, pail, pale, pane, sane, seal/sale, sail, spin, Spain, panel, easel, spaniel, pineapples
Sort for: words ending in **el**:	panel, easel, spaniel
homophones:	pail, pale; pain, pane; sail, sale
*rhyming words:	pain, Spain pane, sane pin, spin
Transfer Words:	crane, remain, twin, begin

*Sort for rhyme and same spelling pattern. Use **crane** and **remain** for reading transfer because you can't be sure which spelling pattern students would use.

Using Words You Know

20 min.

> **Before beginning this month's lessons, help students verbalize that** *Using Words You Know* **is giving them practice in figuring out an unknown word while reading, or coming up with a probable spelling for a word while writing.**

This month's two *Using Words You Know* lessons focus on the **ll** and **ss** final spelling by reviewing words with all five vowels. Here is the procedure (see pages 18-20 for a sample lesson):

1. Display and talk about the words.

2. Identify the spelling patterns.

3. Make as many columns as needed on the board, chart, or transparency and on student papers. Head these with the words and underline the spelling patterns.

4. Show students one-syllable words written on index cards, have them write each word in the column with the same pattern, and have them use the rhyme to pronounce the words.

5. Say one-syllable words and have students decide how to spell them by deciding with which word each rhymes.

6. Repeat the above procedure with longer words.

7. Help students verbalize how words they know help them read and spell lots of other words, including longer words.

Here are two lessons for this month:

Words you know:
a<u>ll</u>, t<u>ell</u>, p<u>ill</u>, r<u>oll</u>, p<u>ull</u>

Words to read:
full, fill, fell, fall, skill, troll, dwell, scroll, cell, sell, stall

Words to spell:
bull, bill, ball, bell, gill, toll, stroll, drill, swell, small

Longer words to read:
waterfall, enroll, basketball, treadmill, misspell, windowsill, eggshell

Longer words to spell:
football, unroll, refill, payroll, doorbell, windmill, shell, snowball

Words you know:

p<u>ass</u>, m<u>ess</u>, k<u>iss</u>, b<u>oss</u>, f<u>uss</u>

Words to read:

muss, moss, miss, mass, floss, brass, dress, Swiss, chess, glass

Words to spell:

grass, cross, toss, stress, hiss, loss, press, bliss, bless, class

Longer words to read:

possess, trespass, discuss, impress, overpass, address, recess, harass

Longer words to spell:

depress, dismiss, express, bypass, confess, unless, underpass

Guess the covered **word.**

Guess the covered **word.**

Guess the Covered Word

20 min.

Guess the Covered Word **lessons provide practice with cross checking by demonstrating to students that guesses based on meaning, beginning letters, or length alone are not very good guesses.** When the reader combines all three, however, and comes up with a word that makes sense, has the same onset, and is about the right length, he can make a very good guess at an unknown word.

Remember to have students make two or three guesses for each word with no letters showing and then to uncover all of the letters up to the vowel. If possible, include some unusually short and long words in the words you cover so that students become sensitive to word length. Here is an example related to foods which has some unusually short and long words:

Food Lover

Eating is one of my very favorite things. I like all kinds of restaurants and all kinds of foods. I love spinach salads. I also like peas on salads. Fruit salads are great if they have lots of watermelon . I love potatoes any way you can cook them. Rice is another of my favorite foods. I love all kinds of fish . I also love cheeseburgers . For dessert, I love all kinds of pie . I also like anything with chocolate in it. I am glad there are so many fabulous foods to eat.

Making These Activities Multilevel

How *Word Sorts and Hunts* Are Multilevel

As traditionally done, *Word Sorts* are not very multilevel. Children begin by sorting for initial letters and then for words with one vowel, two vowels, etc. The *Word Sorts and Hunts* in this book were made multilevel by including some longer words with common patterns and by including some common patterns such as **sure** and **ture** which only occur at the end of longer words.

Limiting the first day's sorting to the most common patterns and one-syllable words, and then increasing to longer words and the patterns found in longer words, provides opportunities for children at all different levels of word knowledge. **By beginning with reading sorts in which the children look at and pronounce the word first, then moving to blind sorts in which they must decide where a word goes before seeing it, and finally doing blind writing sorts in which they must write the word before seeing it, the teacher provides success for struggling readers (most of the time!) and a challenge for the best spellers.**

When you do multilevel *Word Sorts and Hunts*, there is something for all of your children to learn:

- Children who, in earlier grades, didn't understand how vowels work have another chance to figure out the system.

- Other children can transfer what they have learned about vowels to longer words. As children read during the word hunt week, they are on the lookout for the vowel being studied in everything they read. The more common patterns in short words are easily found in lots of words. This provides success for all your children.

- Accelerated readers will be motivated to find examples for the less common patterns so that they can fill up the columns that still have room.

You may want to limit your *Word Sorts and Hunts* to one-syllable words if almost all of your children are struggling, and emphasize the longer words if almost all your students are accelerated. If you have a "motley crew," however, do the lessons as written because they are planned to have "something for everyone."

How the *Word Wall* Is Multilevel

The *Word Wall* meets the needs of a wide range of children. Most of the "tricky" words, such as **because**, **friend**, and **they**, are on the wall and all of your children should be spelling these correctly in everything they write. You also have examples for endings and spelling changes. Expect most of your children to drop **e**, change **y** to **i**, and double consonants when they write words with endings. You should also see children correctly spelling words that begin with the prefix **re-** and end with the suffixes **-ful**, **-less**, **-ly**, and **-en**. If you have been diligent in practicing *Word Wall* words daily and showing your students how example words help them with other words, you should be noticing markedly improved spelling in their first-draft writing.

How the Other Activities Are Multilevel

If you have many struggling readers in your class, continue to emphasize stretching words out to hear all the letters up to the vowel. Remind students how to use patterns from rhyming words to decode and spell other words as they do *Reading/Writing Rhymes, Using Words You Know,* and *Making Words.*

Applying Strategies When Reading and Writing

Throughout this month, the importance of transfer to reading and writing has been reemphasized. If you continue to talk to your students about why the word activities you do are important, and to coach them to use what they know when it is needed, your students will surprise you with their burgeoning independent reading and writing skills in this second half of the year.

FEBRUARY

Month at a Glance

By now, your children should have favorite word activities. Many will love *Making Words* and be anxious to figure out the Secret Word or Mystery Word as soon as they know the letters. *Guess the Covered Word* has added new interest to many of your themes as you are now creating your own examples.

This month, the following activities are provided:
- The *Word Wall* is expanded with 14 new words, including the homophones **by/buy**, **one/won**, and **your/you're**; the compound words **something** and **sometimes**; the **"j"** sound of **g** in **general**; and **-er/-or** suffixes.
- *Using Words You Know* lessons focus on **st** and **tch** final spelling patterns with all five vowels.
- *Guess the Covered Word* extends to a science paragraph on energy.
- *Making Words* lessons use food words.
- *Reading/Writing Rhymes* focuses on long vowels with two common spelling patterns **eal/eel**.
- *Word Sorts and Hunts* focuses on common patterns for **i** and sounds for **y** when it is a vowel.
- Introduce *What Looks Right?* to help develop a visual checking sense with the **ail/ale** pattern.

Here are some time guidelines to consider this month:

Class with Most Children On Grade Level
- 5 minutes *Word Wall* practice daily
- Three 20-minute word lessons each week, including *What Looks Right?, Word Sorts and Hunts, Reading/Writing Rhymes, Using Words You Know, Making Words,* and *Guess the Covered Word*

Class with Most Children Struggling with Grade-Level Material
- 10 minutes *Word Wall* practice daily
- One 20-minute word lesson every day, including *What Looks Right?, Word Sorts and Hunts, Reading/Writing Rhymes, Using Words You Know, Making Words,* and *Guess the Covered Word*

Class with Almost All Children On or Above Grade Level
- 5 minutes *Word Wall* practice daily
- Two 20-minute word lessons each week, picking and choosing from *What Looks Right?, Word Sorts and Hunts, Reading/Writing Rhymes, Using Words You Know, Making Words,* and *Guess the Covered Word*

Word Wall

10 min.

The new words for February include homophones, compound words, an example for the **"j"** sound of **g**, examples for the **un-** prefix and the **-ness** suffix, and some words with the **-er/-or** suffix (meaning "a person or thing that does something"). Here are the words:

by	buy	didn't	doesn't	general	governor	something
sometimes	one	unhappiness	winner	won	your	you're

❶ Add the words to your display. **If you are using different colors, you may be running out of colors for those multiple w words. Repeat colors if needed but be sure to put homophones on different colors.** Attach clues with the number 1 next to **one**, "you are" next to **you're**, and the word "sell" next to **buy**. If you are also using the portable *Word Walls*, give students a new sheet to which the new words (and clues) have been added (see page 159 for reproducibles).

❷ Focus student attention on each word and have students chant it cheerleader style with you. Before cheering for each word, point out helpful clues and illogicalities:

by/buy, one/won, your/you're	By now students should not need any explanation of how the clues you are attaching help them know which word to use. You might point out that they can already spell **one** if they can spell **anyone**.
didn't, doesn't	Students should figure out that these are contractions for **did not** and **does not**. Remember to click and gesture for the apostrophe when cheering.
general	This is an example for the **"j"** sound of **g** and the **al** pattern commonly found at the end of words. Point out that this **al** is also found at the end of the word **usual**.
governor	A **governor** is a person who governs. The suffix **-or** at the end of words often means "a person or thing that does something," as in **actor** and **visitor**.
something, sometimes	These are compound words with **some**.
unhappiness	Here is the word **happy** with the prefix **un-**, making it an opposite and the suffix **-ness.** Third graders know lots of **un-** words, including **unlocked** and **unfair**, and lots of **-ness** words, including **sadness** and **kindness**. Let them explain to you the **i** before the **-ness.**
winner	This is the word **win** with the ending **-er,** meaning "person or thing who does something." The **n** is doubled like **t** in **getting** and **d** in **hidden**.

❸ Use writing clues to have students write each word:

Word Wall Riddles

1. Number 1 is a three-letter number word.

2. Number 2 is the other three-letter word pronounced just like number 1.

3. For number 3, write the opposite of **sell**.

4. For number 4, write the word that means "a person who does something" and ends in **-er.**

5. For number 5, write the word that means "a person who does something" and ends in **-or.**

6. Number 6 starts with a **g** that has a **"j"** sound.

7. For number 7, write the word that has the prefix **un-** and the suffix **-ness.**

Answer Key: 1. **one** 2. **won** 3. **buy** 4. **winner** 5. **governor** 6. **general** 7. **unhappiness**

After students write the words, have them check their own papers by once more chanting the letters aloud, underlining each letter as they say it.

Extending the *Word Wall* to Other Words

Students now have 84 words they are spelling automatically and fluently. They should also be able to spell lots of other words, including these from previous months:

should	would	cause	cities	communities	country	excite
excited	get	laugh	laughing	school	beauty	cover
covers	covered	covering	recover	recovers	recovered	recovering
discovers	discovered	discovering	rough	tough	hope	hopes
hoped	hoping	hopeful	shouldn't	couldn't	anything	everyone
hiding	troubling	writing	written	special	friend	friendlier
friendliest	newer	newest	real	usual	excitedly	beautifully
		hopelessly	hopefully	terribly		

In addition, students should now be able to spell the following:

generally	unhappy	happy	happily	unhappily
happier	happiest	unhappier	unhappiest	anything

Show students how the new prefixes and suffixes can help them spell other words:

- If you can spell **kind, sad,** and **dark,** how would you spell **kindness, sadness,** and **darkness**?
- If you can spell **kind, fair,** and **lock,** how would you spell **unkind, unfair,** and **unlock**?

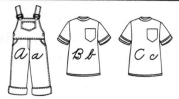 

For **-er/-or** endings, tell students that it is not possible to know which one to use unless they have seen the word before and can remember which one looks right. If they need to know the correct spelling, they can check it in the dictionary. There are many more words spelled **-er** than **-or**. **Farm**, **work**, and **teach** are just three of the numerous examples that add **-er** (to become **farmer**, **worker**, and **teacher**). **Act**, **sail**, and **edit** add **-or** to become **actor**, **sailor**, and **editor**.

If your students enjoy the contests and banner (see page 34), you could do these with **un-**, **-ness**, and **-er/-or**. Be sure to have students check their **-er/-or** words in a dictionary before adding them to the banner.

Reviewing with *Be a Mind Reader*

Most third graders love *Be a Mind Reader*. Remember to make the first clue fairly general and then narrow it down so that there is only one possible word by clue five. Express amazement at all of the students who read your mind and got the word on clue 1, 2, 3 or 4. Here are two examples for this month:

Example One

1. It's in the first half of our *Word Wall*, somewhere between **a** and **m**.

2. It has nine or more letters.

3. It is not a compound word.

4. It does not end in **-ly.**

5. It ends with the suffix **-ful**!

Answer: **beautiful**

Example Two

1. It's in the last half of our *Word Wall*, somewhere between **n** and **z**.

2. It has six or more letters.

3. It is not a contraction.

4. It begins with a **p**.

5. It ends with the suffix **-est,** meaning "most."

Answer: **prettiest**

What Looks Right?

20 min.

In English, words that have the same spelling pattern usually rhyme. If a reader comes to the unknown words **quail** and **stale**, she can easily figure out their pronunciation by accessing the pronunciation associated with other **ail** or **ale** words she can read and spell. The fact that there are two common spelling patterns with the same pronunciation is not a problem when a person is trying to read an unfamiliar-in-print word, but it is a problem when she is trying to spell it. **Quail** and **stale** could as easily be spelled **q-u-a-l-e** and **s-t-a-i-l**. The only way to know which is the correct spelling is to write it one way and see if it "looks right" or check the probable spelling in a dictionary. *What Looks Right?* **lessons help students learn to use these two important self-monitoring spelling strategies.**

What Looks Right? lessons should only be used once students are spelling words by pattern rather than in the one-letter-one-sound way used by beginning spellers. If most of your students are still spelling letter-by-letter, wait until they are pattern spellers before beginning these lessons.

For the first lesson, use the ail/ale pattern. **Decoding and spelling lessons should never last more than 20 minutes.** If students are not familiar with finding words in the dictionary, this activity will take more time. It is time well spent, however, because they need to learn how the dictionary can help them with spellings and meanings. Stop the lesson after 20 minutes, collecting students' papers to continue another day. The first lessons may take three or four sessions, but, as students become faster at finding words, the pace will pick up considerably. Here is a description of the steps in an initial *What Looks Right?* lesson:

❶ Write two words which your students can read and spell, and which have the **ale/ail** patterns. For this lesson, use **whale** and **jail**.

❷ Have students say these words and notice that they rhyme but that they don't have the same spelling pattern. Explain to students that, in English, using a rhyming word to read another word will often work, but that spelling is more complicated because some rhymes have two common spellings. Explain that good spellers use a visual checking strategy. After writing a little-used word, they look at it to see if it "looks right." Ask students if they have ever written a word and realized that it just didn't look right. Explain that if a word doesn't look right, a good speller tries to think of another rhyming word with a different spelling pattern, and writes that one to see if it looks right. Finally, if she needs to be sure of the spelling, she looks it up in a dictionary by looking for it the way she thinks it is spelled. Explain that the activity the class is going to do with called *What Looks Right?* and will help them learn to check on their own spelling the way good spellers do.

3 Create two columns on a chart or overhead and head them with the words **jail** and **whale**. Have the students create these columns on their own papers, writing the words and underlining the spelling patterns **ail** and **ale.** Tell them that there are many words that rhyme with **jail** and **whale** and that you can't tell by just saying a word which spelling pattern it will have. Explain that you are going to say words and write them using both spelling patterns. The students' job is to decide which one looks right to them and write only that one. They will then find the word they wrote in the dictionary to "prove" it is the correct spelling.

4 Say a word that rhymes with **jail** and **whale** and write it both ways, saying, "If **fail** is spelled like **jail**, it will be **f-a-i-l**. If it is spelled like **whale**, it will be **f-a-l-e**." Write these two possible spellings in the appropriate columns. Tell the students to decide which one "looks right" to them and to only write the one they think is correct.

5 Once students have committed to a probable spelling by writing the word in one of the columns, have them use the dictionary to see if that spelling can be found. If they cannot find the one they wrote, then have them look up the other possible spelling. Erase or cross out the spelling you wrote that is not correct and continue with some more examples.

6 The next word is **scale**: "If **scale** is spelled like **jail**, it will be **s-c-a-i-l**. If it is spelled like **whale**, it will be **s-c-a-l-e**." Write the word both ways, have each student write it the way that looks right, and then let students check it in the dictionary.

7 Use these words next, writing each both ways:

trail	nail	stale	snail

Have students commit to a spelling by writing each word in only one column, then have them look in the dictionary to find it.

8 Write **tale** and **tail** in your columns and, without giving away the fact that both are possible spellings, have students commit and use the dictionary to check. When both spellings are found, have someone read the dictionary definitions. Help students see how this wonderful tool, the dictionary, can let them know which word to use when they have two words which are pronounced the same but which have different spellings and meanings. Next write **bail/bale**, **mail/male**, and **pail/pale** and reinforce this notion of how the dictionary helps with sound-alike words.

Looks **Right**

Looks **Right**

9 In the first part of the lesson, you used words students had seen before so they would recognize which "looks right" and know the correct spelling. Now, use some words they probably haven't seen so they will realize that if they haven't seen it before, they can't tell if it looks right and they really need to check the dictionary. Write these words both ways:

frail	quail

After students find these words in the dictionary, have someone read the definitions. Help students create sentences to build some meaning for these words.

10 Explain to students that this checking to see if a word looks right and using a dictionary to check spelling works with longer words, too. Write the following words both ways on the chart. Have students write the one they think is correct and use the dictionary to check.

inhale	toenail	female	detail

When you finally finish this lesson—which may take several 20-minute sessions—your board or overhead will look like the one below.

Have students review these words with you. Help them summarize what good spellers do and don't do. **Good spellers don't spell words one letter at a time. They use the spelling patterns they know from other words.** If a word does not look right, a good speller tries another pattern for that sound. The dictionary helps check probable spellings and lets the writer know which sound-alike word has the meaning he wants.

```
        -ail                          -ale

  jail      pail            whale       pale
  fail      frail           fale        frale
  seail     quail           scale       quale
  trail     inhail          trale       inhale
  nail      toenail         nale        toenale
  stail     femail          stale       female
  snail     detail          snale       detale
  tail      mail            tale        male
  bail                      bale
```

Word Sorts and Hunts

20 min.

This month's word sorting and hunting activities will review all the common patterns for the vowel **i** and the two common sounds for **y** when it is a vowel.

The steps for this lesson are as follows:

1 Use the reproducible sheets on pages 170-174 to make a transparency for yourself and sorting sheets for the students, or create your own. On the first day, each child has a sort sheet and the teacher has a transparency that looks like this:

Other	i	ie	i–e	ir	y	y	tion	sion
give	it	die	nice	bird	my	happy	nation	mansion

2 Have your students fold their sheets so that they can't see the last four columns—**y, y, -tion,** and **-sion.** Cover those four columns on your transparency.

3 Have the children pronounce each of the key words and notice the spelling pattern. Explain that you are going to show them words and they must decide in which column each word fits. To go in a column, the word must have the same spelling pattern and the same sound. Help students see that the word **give** has the **i–e** pattern but cannot go in that column because it does not have the same sound heard in **nice**. The "other" column is where they will put the tricky words—the ones that don't follow the logical patterns. To decide where to put each word, students must both look at the letters and listen to the sounds. Challenge them to not let you "trick them" with some of your tricky words!

4 Show your children 15-20 words which have the vowel **i**. As you show them each word, have them pronounce the word and then write it in the column in which they think it belongs. Choose a child to come write the word in the correct column on your transparency and then continue with the next word. Here are some words for the first day's lesson:

first	with	ripe	shine	hinge	girl
fine	lie	hint	bill	mile	third
bridge	bride	pie	skirt	tire	fish

❺ On the second day, use the same sheet again, uncover the **y** columns, and keep the last two columns covered. Show another 15-20 words and have students sort them into the first seven columns. Include some words with more than one syllable and help children focus on the syllable that has the **i** in it. Be sure to have students pronounce each word before writing it and remind them to watch for tricky words. They can't just look at the letters, but must also listen for the sounds. Here are some words to use:

sky	party	slice	gym	blister	curly
admire	birth	circus	butterfly	untie	sizzle
blizzard	forgive	multiply	pretty	exercise	alive

❻ On the third day, use all columns. Show students another 15-20 words and have them pronounce and then write them in the appropriate column. Try these words:

vacation	pension	arrive	motion	friend	sir
tie	rely	porcupine	supply	type	ski
worry	circle	strike	station	cousin	tension
		marry			

At the end of the third day, your chart should look like this:

Other	i	ie	i-e	ir	y	y	tion	sion
give	it	die	nice	bird	my	happy	nation	masion
hinge	with	lie	ripe	first	sky	party	vacation	pension
bridge	hint	pie	shine	girl	butterfly	curly	motion	tension
gym	bill	untie	fine	third	multiply	pretty	station	
forgive	fish	tie	mile	skirt	rely	worry		
friend	blister		bride	birth	supply	marry		
type	sizzle		tire	circus				
ski	blizzard		slice	sir				
	cousin		admire	circle				
	multiply		exercise					
			alive					
			arrive					
			porcupine					
			strike					

❼ On the fourth day, do a blind sort. Give the children a new sorting sheet, just like the one they used the first three days, and use a new transparency. Pick 15-20 words already sorted but say each word without showing it. Have each child indicate where she thinks it belongs by putting a finger on the column. When the children are pointing at the column, show them the word and have them write it where it belongs.

❽ The final activity for the fifth day is a blind writing sort. Again, choose 15-20 words already sorted on days 1-3 but, instead of showing the word, say the word and have students try to write it in the correct column before you show it. Depending of the level of your class, you may want to use some of the easier words on this day. If you use some of the more sophisticated words, praise students for writing them in the correct columns even if they are not spelled correctly. Have students correct any incorrect letters after someone writes the word on the transparency. By the end of the fifth day, all students should have a much better notion of some common spelling patterns for the vowels **i** and **y**.

❾ Next week, move the children from word sorting to word hunting. Give them another clean sheet with the columns. Tell them that they have one week to find other words that fit the patterns and write them or their sheets. Encourage them to hunt for words everywhere—around the room; on signs; in books they are reading; and while reading in science, social studies, and math. Have them keep their lists secret and encourage them to gather as many words as possible—especially big words—to contribute to the final sort.

❿ For the final sort, attach a large piece of butcher paper across the chalkboard. Set up columns just as they were on the original sort sheets, using a different color permanent marker for each. Let children take turns coming to the front of the class, writing one word in its correct column, pronouncing that word, and, for an obscure word, using it in a sentence. Words can be added until the children run out of words or until there is no more room in a particular column. If possible, hang the butcher paper somewhere in the room and encourage your students to continue to look for words for any columns that still have room.

Reading/Writing Rhymes

20 min.

This month's lessons work with the **eal/eel** and **eap/eep** patterns to provide more examples of how some long vowels have two common spelling patterns.

Here are some words for this month's charts:

<u>eal</u>	<u>eel</u>
meal	eel
deal	feel
heal	heel
veal	wheel
steal	steel
real	reel
seal	kneel
zeal	peel
peal	keel
teal	

ordeal, oatmeal, appeal, conceal, ideal, unreal, cartwheel

*Oldsmobile®, automobile

<u>eap</u>	<u>eep</u>
cheap	cheep
heap	beep
leap	creep
reap	sleep
	deep
	jeep
	weep
	keep
	sweep
	sheep
	steep
	peep
	seep
asleep	

Making Words

20 min.

This month, there are three *Making Words* lessons in which the secret word is something most third graders like to eat.

Here are three *Making Words* lessons for February. (The / indicates words that can be made by simply rearranging the same letters.)

Lesson One:	**Secret Word: Snickers®**
Letters on strip:	e i c k n r s s
Make:	in, ski, ice, nice, rice, rink, sink/skin, sick, rise, risen/rinse, skier, sicken, Snickers®
Sort for: related words:	ski, skier rise, risen sick, sicken
rhyming words:	in, skin ice, nice, rice rink, sink
Transfer Words:	advice, Berlin, shrink, price

Lesson One:	**Secret Word: Cheerios®**
Letters on strip:	e e i o c h r s
Make:	is, his, rich, hero, echo, core, score, shore, chore, cheer, sheer, heroes, echoes, riches, Cheerios®
Sort for: related words:	hero, heroes echo, echoes rich, riches (**es** ending)
rhyming words:	core, score, shore, chore cheer, sheer is, his
Transfer Words:	reindeer, adore, restore, steer

Lesson Three:	**Secret Word: pretzels**
Letters on strip:	e e l p r s t z
Make:	set, pet, pets/step/pest, rest, zest, steep, sleep, slept, reset, spree, pester, seltzer, pretzels
Sort for: related words:	set, reset pest, pester sleep, slept
rhyming words:	set, pet, reset pest, rest, zest steep, sleep
Transfer Words:	request, invest, upset, jeep

Using Words You Know

20 min.

This month's *Using Words You Know* lessons focus on the **st** and **tch** final spellings by reviewing words with all five vowels. Here are the steps (see pages 18-20 for a sample lesson):

1. Display and talk about the words.

2. Identify the spelling patterns.

3. Make as many columns as needed on the board, chart, or transparency and on student papers. Head these with the words and underline the spelling patterns.

4. Show students one-syllable words written on index cards. Have students write each word in the correct column and use the rhyme to pronounce the words.

5. Say one-syllable words and have students decide how to spell them by deciding with which word each rhymes.

6. Repeat the above procedure with longer words.

7. Help students verbalize how words they know help them read and spell lots of other words, including longer words.

Here are two *Using Words You Know* lessons for February:

Words you know:
f<u>ast</u>, b<u>est</u>, l<u>ist</u>, c<u>ost</u>, j<u>ust</u>

Words to read:
lost, trust, twist, gust, cast, wrist, chest, must, west, blast

Words to spell:
crust, frost, rust, mist, dust, past, fist, vest, crest, last

Longer words to read:
adjust, sawdust, assist, request, mistrust, checklist, exist, suggest, broadcast

Longer words to spell:
defrost, unjust, insist, forecast, disgust, resist, contest, protest

---

Words you know:

c<u>atch</u>, str<u>etch</u>, p<u>itch</u>, n<u>otch</u>, cr<u>utch</u>

Words to read:

batch, botch, clutch, witch, twitch, sketch, match, Dutch, hitch

Words to spell:

stitch, hutch, itch, blotch, switch, fetch, ditch, scratch, latch

Longer words to read:

topnotch, bewitch, homestretch, mismatch

Longer words to spell:

unhitch, dispatch, hopscotch, unlatch

Finished charts should look like this:

f<u>ast</u>	**b<u>est</u>**	**l<u>ist</u>**	**c<u>ost</u>**	**j<u>ust</u>**
cast	chest	twist	lost	trust
blast	west	wrist	frost	gust
past	vest	mist	defrost	must
last	crest	fist		crust
broadcast	request	assist		rust
forecast	suggest	checklist		dust
	contest	exist		adjust
	protest	insist		sawdust
		resist		mistrust
				unjust
				disgust

c<u>atch</u>	**str<u>etch</u>**	**p<u>itch</u>**	**n<u>otch</u>**	**cr<u>utch</u>**
batch	sketch	witch	botch	clutch
match	fetch	twitch	blotch	Dutch
scratch	homestretch	hitch	topnotch	hutch
latch		stitch	hopscotch	
mismatch		itch		
dispatch		switch		
unlatch		ditch		
		bewitch		
		unhitch		

Guess the covered word.

Guess the covered word.

Guess the Covered Word

20 min.

For February, consider using paragraphs connected to class science units. This one fits into the popular third-grade science topic of energy:

Energy

We get energy from many **different** sources. Our lights, **televisions**, and dishwashers get their energy from electricity. Some houses also get **heat** from electricity. Other houses are heated by **gas**, oil, or solar energy. Most of our cars, trucks, and **buses** get their energy from gasoline. There are also some electric **vehicles**. Some people believe that in the future our cars will run on **solar** energy. In some places, **nuclear** power plants supply most of the energy needs. In many parts of the world, energy is created from **wind** and water.

Making These Activities Multilevel

How *What Looks Right?* Is Multilevel

Think about the progression of a *What Looks Right?* lesson and you will see many opportunities for your struggling readers to begin to figure out the system, as well as challenges to keep your best readers on their toes.

- **The first words in each lesson are words for which many students will recognize the correct spelling.** When they choose the correct spelling and then find it in the dictionary, they experience the success that motivates increased engagement.

- All lessons work with the concept of rhyme and the idea that words which rhyme usually have the same spelling pattern. **If students are still unsure about how to figure out unknown words in reading, the "think of a word you know with the same pattern and make it rhyme" decoding strategy is reinforced in every *What Looks Right?* lesson.**

- **Students who understand how patterns help them read words will begin to see that to spell words correctly, they have to use patterns but they also have to start noticing which pattern looks right.**

- **All students get practice in finding words in the dictionary and using the dictionary to check on a probable spelling.** Accelerated third graders soon realize how the dictionary helps them know which word to use when they have two words which are pronounced the same but which have different spellings and meanings.

- Including some less common words in each lesson lets **your advanced students come to realize that, if they haven't seen a word before, they can't tell if it looks right so they really need to check the dictionary.** Each lesson ends with some longer words to further challenge your fast word learners.

How the Other Activities Are Multilevel

The *Word Wall* should be helping students spell even more words correctly with the addition of some additional homophones and contractions, and with **governor** and **winner** as examples for the **-or** and **-er** endings.

Notice how some of the transfer words in *Making Words* lessons have been two-syllable words to reinforce the idea that rhyming patterns work for longer words, too. Remember that you can modify lessons to emphasize shorter or longer words if your class is "heavy" on either end. Including the range of words provided for every lesson will make your lessons more multilevel if you have a wide range of students.

Applying Strategies When Reading and Writing

Continue reminding students to use their strategies while reading and writing:

- Before students write, have them read the *Word Wall* words quickly and remind them why the words are on the wall and being practiced.
- When students have finished writing, have them reread their pieces looking for *Word Wall* words, as well as words that don't look right. Help them to think of other words they know with different spelling patterns, and see if writing the word that way results in a word that "looks right."
- Before students read, remind them that everyone sees new words in their reading. If they will say all of the letters in an unfamiliar word, their brains will search out other words with similar patterns—rhymes, roots, prefixes, and suffixes—which will help them come up with a pronunciation. Remind students to always check their pronunciation to make sure it makes sense and "sounds right."
- Help students share their spelling and decoding success stories with other students.

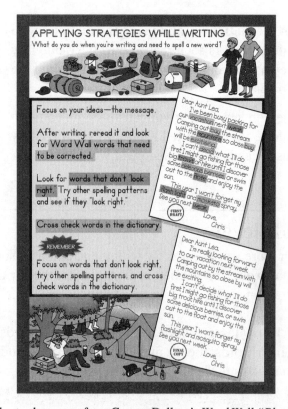

*Charts shown are from Carson-Dellosa's *Word Wall "Plus" for Third Grade* (CD-2504).

MARCH

Month at a Glance

By now, your class should be springing into many of the activities with ease. They now know the routines and, if your pace is brisk, all are challenged and succeed. *Word Wall* words are showing up correctly spelled in first-draft writing—your efforts are paying off.

The following will be suggested for March:
- The *Word Wall* is expanded with 14 more words, including the homophones **threw/through** and **wear/where**; the contractions **that's**, **it's**, **I'm**, and **we're**; and the suffixes **-tion** and **-sion**.
- *Using Words You Know* lessons focus on **ng** and **nk** in final spelling with **a, i, o,** and **u**.
- *Guess the Covered Word* explores the figure being carved in the Black Hills of South Dakota.
- *Making Words* lessons expand to science and electricity.
- *Reading/Writing Rhymes* explores spelling patterns with **oan/one** and **ute/oot**.
- *Word Sorts and Hunts* reviews common patterns for **e**.
- *What Looks Right?* explores **ear/eer** patterns.
- A new activity, *Rivet*, is introduced. This activity teaches students to pay close attention to all letters in unfamiliar words.

Here are some time guidelines to consider this month:

Class with Most Children On Grade Level
- 5 minutes *Word Wall* practice daily
- Three 20-minute word lessons each week, including *What Looks Right?, Word Sorts and Hunts, Reading/Writing Rhymes, Using Words You Know, Making Words,* and *Guess the Covered Word*

Class with Most Children Struggling with Grade-Level Material
- 10 minutes *Word Wall* practice daily
- One 20-minute word lesson every day, including *What Looks Right?, Word Sorts and Hunts, Reading/Writing Rhymes, Using Words You Know, Making Words,* and *Guess the Covered Word*

Class with Almost All Children On or Above Grade Level
- 5 minutes *Word Wall* practice daily
- Two 20-minute word lessons each week, picking and choosing from *What Looks Right?, Word Sorts and Hunts, Reading/Writing Rhymes, Using Words You Know, Making Words,* and *Guess the Covered Word*

Word Wall

10 min.

Here are the new words for March:

another	confusion	**I'm**	its	it's	question	that's
threw	through	vacation	we're	wear	where	with

❶ Add the words to your display. If you are using different colors, you may be running out of colors for those multiple **w** and **t** words. Repeat colors if needed, but be sure to put homophones on different colors. Attach clues with "it is" next to **it's**, a picture of a baseball cap next to **wear**, "we are" next to **we're**, and a picture of a baseball next to **threw**. If you are also using the portable *Word Walls*, give students a new sheet with the new words (and clues) added (see page 160 for a reproducible).

❷ Focus student attention on each word and have students chant it, cheerleader style, with you. Before cheering for each word, point out helpful clues and illogicalities:

another	Students should realize this is a compound word made up of **an** and **other**.
confusion	This is the word **confuse** with the **e** dropped and the suffix **-sion** added. Although the end of the word sounds like it should be spelled **s-h-u-n**, long words that end like this are always spelled **s-i-o-n** or **t-i-o-n**. A reader can't tell which spelling is correct unless she has seen it before and remembers if it looks right, or checks it in the dictionary.
its/it's, threw/through	By now, students should not need any explanation of how the clues you are attaching help them know which word to use. Help them use **its**, **it's**, **threw**, and **through** in sentences. There is no logic for **through** to be spelled like **enough**!
I'm, that's	Students should figure out that these are contractions for **I am** and **that is**. Make sure students notice the uppercase **I** in **I'm**. Remember to click and gesture for the apostrophe when cheering.
question	This is an example for **qu** and the ending **-tion**.
vacation	Here is another example for the **-tion** ending.
we're, wear, where	Clues should help determine which one to use when writing; **wear** and **where** are illogical spellings which don't follow the patterns.
with	This is a logical word but still often misspelled.

3 Use writing clues to have students write each word:

> ### *Word Wall* Riddles
>
> 1. Number 1 is a four-letter **w** word that fits in this sentence: Do you want fries _____ that?
>
> 2. Number 2 is a contraction that always needs a capital letter.
>
> 3. For number 3, write the seven-letter compound word that rhymes with **brother**.
>
> 4. For number 4, write the five-letter word that tells something you did with a ball.
>
> 5. For number 5, write the other word that is pronounced just like the word you wrote for number 4.
>
> 6. The word for number 6 is a contraction for **we are**.
>
> 7. The word for number 7 is a contraction for **that is**.
>
> Answer Key: 1. **with** 2. **I'm** 3. **another** 4. **threw** 5. **through** 6. **we're** 7. **that's**

After students write the words, have them check their own papers by once more chanting the letters aloud, underlining each letter as they say it.

4 Throughout the month, review words by cheering, writing, and (when students have been good!) playing a few rounds of *Be a Mind Reader* (see page 76). Don't give up on writing "WW" when needed, although the need for that should be lessening and you—and your students—should be reaping the rewards of your determination!

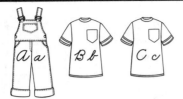 

Extending the *Word Wall* to Other Words

Students now have 98 *Word Wall* words they are spelling automatically and fluently. They should also be able to spell lots of other words, including these from previous months:

should	would	cause	cities	communities	country
excite	excited	get	laugh	laughing	school
beauty	cover	covers	covered	covering	recover
recovers	recovered	recovering	discovers	discovered	discovering
rough	tough	hope	hopes	hoped	hoping
hopeful	shouldn't	couldn't	anything	everyone	hiding
troubling	writing	written	special	friend	friendlier
friendliest	newer	newest	real	usual	excitedly
beautifully	hopelessly	hopefully	terribly	generally	unhappy
happy	happily	unhappily	happier	happiest	unhappier
	unhappiest	anything			

In addition, students should now be able to spell the following:

other	confuse	confused	confusing
questioning	questioned	vacationing	vacationed

For **-tion/-sion** endings, tell students that it is not possible to know which one to use unless they have seen the word before and can remember which ending looks right. **If they need to know the correct spelling, they should check it in the dictionary.** One thing they can be sure of is that long words that end like this are not spelled s-h-u-n!

If your students enjoy the contests and banner (see page 34), do these with **-sion/-tion**. Be sure to have students check their words in a dictionary before adding them to the banner.

Rivet

When children read, they are going to come across many words they have never before seen in print. **When facing a new word, a good reader looks at all of the letters in the word, in sequence, to figure out the word.** Many struggling readers just take a quick glance at an unfamiliar word and then look away, without looking at all of the letters. *Rivet* is an activity designed to get students in the habit of paying close attention to all the letters in an unfamiliar word.

Use *Rivet* to introduce unfamiliar words important to a selection children are going to read. (It is called *Rivet* because, unlike more traditional vocabulary introduction activities in which children are often seen staring out the window or at their shoes, all of the children's eyes are riveted to the board as the teacher slowly writes the letters of the words.) Here is the procedure:

❶ To prepare for a *Rivet* activity, **read the selection the children will read and pick six to eight important words, with a particular emphasis on polysyllabic words and important names.** This example lesson uses the following words:

railroad	**package**	**Florida**	**seashell**
Thursday	**embankment**	**surprise**	**Miss Jones**

❷ Begin the activity by writing numbers and drawing lines on the board to indicate how many letters each word has. Have the students draw the same number of lines on scrap paper. Your board and their papers at the beginning of the *Rivet* activity should look like this:

1. _ _ _ _ _ _ _ _

2. _ _ _ _ _ _ _

3. _ _ _ _ _ _ _

4. _ _ _ _ _ _ _ _

5. _ _ _ _ _ _ _

6. _ _ _ _ _ _ _ _ _

7. _ _ _ _ _ _ _

8. _ _ _ _ _ _ _ _ _

❸ Fill in the letters of the first word one at a time. Have the students write them as you do and encourage them to guess the word as soon as they think they know the word. (Students are guessing the word—not the letters.) Most students could not guess the word when the board looks like this:

> 1. **r a i _ _ _ _ _**

Many students, however, will guess with a few more letters:

> 1. **r a i l r _ _ _**

Once someone has guessed the correct word, ask him to help you finish spelling it. Write it on the board as students write it on their papers.

❹ Begin writing the letters of the second word, pausing for just a second after each letter:

> 1. **r a i l r o a d**
> 2. **p a _ _ _ _ _**

The attention of all the students is generally "riveted" to each added letter, and with a few more letters many students will guess the word:

> 1. **r a i l r o a d**
> 2. **p a c k a _ _**

If the students are right, have them help you finish spelling the word. If they give you an incorrect guess, continue writing letters until someone guesses the correct word.

❺ Continue in this fashion until all of the words have been completely written and correctly guessed. Here is what the board and student's papers should look like when all words have been introduced:

> 1. **r a i l r o a d**
> 2. **p a c k a g e**
> 3. **F l o r i d a**
> 4. **s e a s h e l l**
> 5. **T h u r s d a y**
> 6. **e m b a n k m e n t**
> 7. **s u r p r i s e**
> 8. **M i s s   J o n e s**

RIVET

RIVET

6 Once all of the words have been identified, have the students use them to predict some of the events in the story. Encourage divergent predictions by asking questions which lead students to consider alternative possibilities.

- One child may say: "Miss Jones brought a surprise package to Florida."

- Another child may suggest: "Miss Jones found a surprise package near a railroad embankment."

- Still another child may say: "The package found by the railroad embankment belonged to Miss Jones."

Encourage as many predictions as possible. As student make these predictions, they are thinking about what might happen and using key words they will soon be reading in the selection.

7 After the students have read the selection, use the key words to review their predictions and talk about what actually happened. Be sure to let the students know that you are not just interested in "the right answer." You may want to say something like, "That didn't happen, but it could have, and it might have made a more interesting story."

What Looks Right?

20 min.

Continue using the *What Looks Right?* lesson format. **Remember that each lesson will take several days until students get quicker at using the dictionary to find words and check spelling and meaning. Remember also that this is a crucial strategy, so it is worth the time investment.**

This month's lesson uses the **ear/eer** patterns. The steps for the lesson are as follows:

1. Write two words on the board which your students can read and spell and which have the patterns.

2. Have students say these words and notice that they rhyme but that they don't have the same spelling pattern.

3. Create two columns on a board or overhead and head them with the words, underlining the spelling patterns. Have the students create these columns on their own papers, writing the words and underlining the spelling patterns.

4. As you say each word, write it both ways. Students should write it the way that looks right to them and then check the word by finding it in the dictionary.

5. Once the correct spelling is verified, erase or cross out the spelling you wrote that is not correct. Continue with the next word.

6. End the lesson by having students review the words with you. Help them summarize what good spellers do—and don't do. Good spellers don't spell words one letter at a time. They use the spelling patterns they know from other words. If a word does not look right, a good speller tries another pattern for that sound. The dictionary helps him check the probable spelling and decide which sound-alike word has the desired meaning.

Here are the words for this month's lesson. The finished chart should look like this:

year	cheer
tear	~~teer~~
fear	~~feer~~
near	~~neer~~
~~stear~~	steer
clear	~~cleer~~
gear	~~geer~~
dear	deer
~~jear~~	jeer
~~vear~~	veer
spear	~~speer~~
~~smear~~	sneer
smear	~~smeer~~
shear	sheer
rear	~~reer~~
appear	~~appeer~~
~~reindear~~	reindeer
~~enginear~~	engineer
~~pionear~~	pioneer
	*here

Word Sorts and Hunts

This month's word sorting and hunting activities will review the common patterns for the vowel **e**. The steps for this lesson are as follows:

❶ Use the reproducible sheets on pages 170-174 to make a transparency for yourself and sorting sheets for the students, or create your own. On the first day, each child has a sort sheet and the teacher has a transparency that looks like this:

<u>Other</u>	<u>e</u>	<u>e</u>	<u>ee</u>	<u>ea</u>	<u>ea</u>	<u>er</u>	<u>ew</u>	<u>le</u>
earth	he	pet	tree	eat	bread	her	new	little

❷ Have students fold their sheets so that they can't see the last three columns—**er**, **ew**, and **le**. Cover those columns on your transparency, as well.

❸ Have the children pronounce each of the key words and notice the spelling pattern. Explain that you will to show words and they must decide in which column each word fits. To go in a column, the word must have the same spelling pattern and the same sound. Help students see that the word **earth** has the **ea** pattern but cannot go in either of those columns because it does not have the same sound as **eat** or **bread**. The "other" column is where students will put the tricky words—the ones that don't follow the logical patterns. To decide where to put each word, students must look at the letters and listen to the sounds. Challenge them not to let you "trick them" with some of your tricky words!

❹ Show your children 15-20 words which have the vowel **e**. As you show each word, have students pronounce the word and then write it in the column in which they think it belongs. Choose a child to come write the word in the correct column on your transparency, then continue with the next word. Here are some words for the first day:

tea	set	she	men	east	each
mean	them	head	seat	cheat	least
chest	death	sweet	sweat	bent	bee
					be

❺ On the second day, use the same sheet again, uncover the **er** and **ew** columns, and keep the **le** column covered. Show another 15-20 words and have students sort them into the columns. Include some words with more than one syllable and help children focus on the syllable that has the **e** in it. Be sure to have students pronounce each word before writing it and remind them to watch for tricky words. They can't just look at the letters but must also listen for the sounds. Here are the words for the second day:

dew	magnet	evil	garden	danger	question
cashews	brother	grandmother	chew	news	chef
sixteen	squeak	threat	weapon	person	speech

❻ On the third day, use all columns. Show students another 15-20 words, such as the ones below, and have students pronounce and then write them in the appropriate columns.

ideal	uncle	shrewd	complex	title	perform
alphabet	fable	relax	angle	daydream	gentle
cartwheel	settle	speedy	bundle	terminal	comfortable

❼ On the fourth day, do a blind sort. Give the children a new sorting sheet just like the one they used the first three days, and use a new transparency. Pick 15-20 words already sorted but say each word without showing it. Have the children indicate where they think it belongs by putting a finger on the column. When the children are pointing at the column, show them the word and have them write it where it belongs.

❽ The final activity for the fifth day is a blind writing sort. Again, choose 15-20 words already sorted on days 1-3 but, instead of showing the word, say the word and have students try to write it in the correct column before you show it.

Depending of the level of your class, you may want to use some of the easier words on this fifth day. If you use more sophisticated words, praise students for writing them in the correct columns even if they are not spelled correctly. Have students correct any incorrect letters after someone writes the word on your transparency. By the end of the fifth day, all students should have a much better notion of some of the common spelling patterns for the vowel **e**.

Here is how your completed chart should look:

Other earth	e he	e pet	ee tree	ea eat	ea bread	er her	ew new	le little
she	set	sweet	tea	head	danger	dew	uncle
be	men	bee	east	death	brother	cashews	title
evil	them	sixteen	each	sweat	grandmother	chew	fable
relax	chest	speech	mean	threat	person	news	angle
	bent	cartwheel	seat	weapon	perform	shrewd	gentle
	magnet	speedy	cheat		terminal		settle
	garden		least				bundle
	question		squeak				comfortable
	chef		ideal				
	complex		daydream				
	alphabet						
	gentle						
	settle						

9 Next week, move the children from word sorting to word hunting. Give them another clean sheet with the columns. Tell them that they have one week to find other words that fit the patterns and write them on their sheets. Encourage them to hunt for words everywhere—around the room; on signs; in books they are reading; and while reading in science, social studies, and math. Have them keep their lists secret and encourage them to gather as many words as possible—especially big words—to contribute to the final sort.

10 For the final sort, attach a huge piece of butcher paper across the chalkboard. Set up columns just as they were on the original sort sheets, using a different color permanent marker for each. Let children take turns coming to the front of the class and writing one word in its correct column, pronouncing that word, and, for an obscure word, using it in a sentence. Words can be added until the children run out of words or until there is no more room in a particular column. If possible, hang the butcher paper somewhere in the room and encourage students to continue to look for words for any columns that still have room.

Reading/Writing Rhymes

20 min.

Lessons for this month include words with the **oan/one** and **ute/oot** spelling patterns.

Here are some words for this month's charts:

oan	**one**
moan	bone
groan	phone
Joan	cone
loan	lone
stone	clone
zone	tone
drone	

tombstone, trombone, alone, microphone

*grown, known

ute	**oot**
flute	boot
brute	hoot
jute	loot
mute	shoot
	scoot
	snoot
	toot
	root

salute, pollute, parachute, substitute, offshoot, uproot

*suit, fruit

Making Words

20 min.

This month, there are three *Making Words* lessons in which the secret words connect to the science topic of electricity.

Here are three *Making Words* lessons for March. (The **/** indicates words that can be made by simply rearranging the same letters. For detailed instructions, see pages 35-39.)

Lesson One:	**Secret Word:** electricity
Letters on strip:	e e i i c c l r t t y
Make:	cry, try, ice, rice, city, title, elect, cycle, circle, icicle, recycle, tricycle, electric, electricity
Sort for: related words:	electric, electricity ice, icicle cycle, recycle, tricycle
words ending in **le**:	title, cycle, circle, icicle, recycle, tricycle
rhyming words:	cry, try ice, rice
Transfer Words:	reply, twice, spry, slice

Lesson Two:	**Secret Word:** batteries
Letters on strip:	a e e i b r s t t
Make:	art/rat, rate, east, beast/baste, taste/state, better, batter, bitter, rebate, artist, treaties, batteries
Sort for: related words:	art, artist
y changed to **i** and **es** added:	batteries, treaties
rhyming words:	rate, state, rebate east, beast baste, taste
Transfer Words:	debate, least, paste, feast

Lesson Three:		**Secret Word: magnetic**
Letters on strip:		a e i c g m n t
Make:		eat, act, age, cage, came, game, tame/team, magic, manic, anemic, eating, acting, magnet, magnetic
Sort for:	related words:	act, acting eat, eating magnet, magnetic
	words ending in **ic**:	magic, manic, anemic, magnetic
	rhyming words:	age, cage game, name, tame
Transfer Words:		became, stage, shame, rage

Using Words You Know

20 min.

This month's *Using Words You Know* lessons focus on the **ng** and **nk** final spellings by reviewing words with **a, i, o, and u**.

Here are the steps for a *Using Words You Know* lesson (see page 18-20 for a sample lesson):

1. Display and talk about the words.

2. Identify the spelling patterns.

3. Make as many columns as needed on the board, chart, or transparency and on student papers. Head these with the words and underline the spelling patterns.

4. Show students one-syllable words written on index cards. Have them write each in the column showing the same pattern and use the rhyme to pronounce the words.

5. Say one-syllable words and have students decide how to spell them by deciding with which word each rhymes.

6. Repeat the above procedure with longer words.

7. Help students verbalize how words they know help them read and spell lots of other words, including longer words.

Here are two *Using Words You Know* lessons for March:

Words you know:
hang, king, song, stung

Words to read:
tang, lung, wrong, rung, sling, spring, throng, bang, fang

Words to spell:
sung, sing, string, strong, strung, swing, swung, gang

Longer words to read:
everything, along, earring, boomerang

Longer words to spell:
nothing, belong, anything, mustang, something

Words you know:
bank, pink, junk

Words to read:
skunk, blink, blank, plank, sunk, dunk, shrink, crank

Words to spell:
trunk, flunk, chunk, think, thank, prank, bunk, hunk, Hank

Longer words to read:
kerplunk, gangplank, chipmunk, icerink

Longer words to spell:
uplink, outrank, rethink

Finished charts should look like this:

hang	**king**	**song**	**stung**
tang	sling	wrong	lung
bang	spring	throng	rung
fang	sing	strong	sung
gang	string	along	strung
boomerang	swing	belong	swung
mustang	everything		
	earring		
	nothing		
	anything		
	something		

bank	**pink**	**junk**
blank	blink	skunk
plank	shrink	sunk
crank	think	dunk
thank	icerink	trunk
prank	uplink	flunk
Hank	rethink	chunk
gangplank		bunk
outrank		hunk
		kerplunk
		chipmunk

Guess the covered word.

Guess the covered word.

Guess the Covered Word

20 min.

Do your students know about the new figure being carved in the Black Hills of South Dakota? This *Guess the Covered Word* paragraph was inspired by an article in *USA Today*®. If your students are intrigued by this, they could find more information through a search on the Internet.

New Sculpture in the Black Hills

For years, people have marvelled at the faces of four **presidents** carved into Mount Rushmore in South Dakota. Now, there is another face to see in the **Black** Hills. Work on the face of Crazy Horse, a famous Lakota Indian chief, began over **fifty** years ago. The face of Crazy Horse is **huge**. It is taller than the **Washington** Monument. Each eye **measures** eighteen feet across. All four Mount Rushmore faces could fit inside the **face** of Crazy Horse. The carving is not **finished**. **Sculptors** are now busy carving Crazy Horse's horse. More than one **million** visitors have already paid the $7.00 visitor fee to visit the Crazy Horse **Memorial** and Indian Museum.

Making These Activities Multilevel

The *Word Wall* should be helping students spell even more words correctly with the addition of some additional homophones and contractions, with **confusion** as an example for **con-** and **-sion**, and with **vacation** and **question** as examples for **-tion**. Students should be spelling many more words correctly as they use all the *Word Wall* examples. You may want to point out that students can't always be sure whether a word will end in **-or** or **-er**, **-tion** or **-sion**, but that they can use the strategies of seeing if a word looks right and checking in the dictionary to find out.

Remember that you can modify lessons to emphasize shorter or longer words if your class is "heavy" on either end, but including the range of words in every lesson will make your lessons more multilevel if you have a wide range of students.

Applying Strategies When Reading and Writing

By now you should be seeing some definite improvement in students' contextual spelling and decoding. **Continue to urge them to read their writing before putting it up each day, looking for *Word Wall* words and other words that don't look right.** You might want them each to find one word each day which they don't think they have spelled correctly and use their dictionary skills to find the appropriate spelling. If possible, have students do some of their writing on a computer with a spell check program. Have them use the feature that allows the computer to suggest a possible spelling for the misspelled word. **Help them see that the computer can search through its store of words and find similarly spelled words just as they have been learning to do.**

When students are reading, encourage them to say each letter of an unfamiliar word, search their mental word stores for similar words, and check pronunciation with context. Each day, ask them to share one word from the day's reading selection which they decoded using these strategies, and let them "brag about" how they got it! Challenge students to find big words they can decode in their reading and have them explain how the prefixes and suffixes they have learned help them.

Month at a Glance

As you introduce the last of the third-grade *Word Wall* words, you notice that all students have made great strides in using what they know. They not only spell the words on the wall, but use them to spell related words. There is daily evidence that they are applying what they have learned in the various strategies as they read and write.

This month, the following will be suggested:

- The *Word Wall* will be expanded with 12 final words, including **weather/whether** and **whole/hole**. *The Wheel*, an activity to review *Word Wall* words, is introduced.
- *Using Words You Know* is expanded to team competition with fairly uncommon words.
- The *Guess the Covered Word* lesson features "fascinating facts" about koalas.
- *Making Words* lessons this month have car names as secret words.
- *Reading/Writing Rhymes* lessons use rhymes with three spelling patterns: **are/air/ear** and **ue/ew/oo**.
- *Word Sorts and Hunts* explores common patterns for **a**.
- *What Looks Right?* focuses on **oak/oke** patterns.

Here are some time guidelines to consider this month:

Class with Most Children On Grade Level

- 5 minutes *Word Wall* practice daily
- Three 20-minute word lessons each week, including *What Looks Right?*, *Word Sorts and Hunts*, *Reading/Writing Rhymes*, *Using Words You Know*, *Making Words*, and *Guess the Covered Word*

Class with Most Children Struggling with Grade-Level Material

- 10 minutes *Word Wall* practice daily
- One 20-minute word lesson every day, including *What Looks Right?*, *Word Sorts and Hunts*, *Reading/Writing Rhymes*, *Using Words You Know*, *Making Words*, and *Guess the Covered Word*

Class with Almost All Children On or Above Grade Level

- 5 minutes *Word Wall* practice daily
- Two 20-minute word lessons each week, picking and choosing from *What Looks Right?*, *Word Sorts and Hunts*, *Reading/Writing Rhymes*, *Using Words You Know*, *Making Words*, and *Guess the Covered Word*

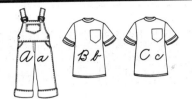

Word Wall

10 min.

This month, add the final 12 *Word Wall* words for a grand total of 110!

almost	also	always	impossible	independent	lovable
thought	were	weather	whether	whole	hole

❶ Add the words to your display. If you are using different colors, you may be running out of colors for those multiple **w** and **t** words. **Repeat colors if needed, but be sure to put homophones on different colors.** Attach clues, such as a picture of a cloud for **weather** and a doughnut hole with an arrow pointed to the hole for **hole**. If you are also using the portable *Word Walls*, give students a sheet with the new words (and clues) added (see page 161 for a reproducible).

❷ Focus student attention on each word and have students chant it, cheerleader style, with you. Before "cheering" for each word, point out helpful clues and illogicalities:

almost, also, always	All of these are words in which the first syllable would logically be spelled **all**.
impossible	This is **possible** with the prefix **im-** making it an opposite. Other **im-** opposites include **impatient** and **immature**. Point out the familiar **le** pattern at the end of **impossible**.
independent	This is **depend** with the suffix **-ent** and the prefix **in-** making it an opposite. Other **in-** opposite words include **insecure** and **incorrect**.
lovable	**Lovable** is **love** with the suffix **-able**. Students should notice that the **e** is dropped when **-able** is added.
thought	This is an illogical spelling but the same pattern is used in other words, including **ought**, **bought**, and **brought**.
were	Here is another **w** word with an illogical spelling.
weather/whether, hole/whole	Clues should help determine which one to use when writing.

3 Use writing clues to have students write each word:

> ### *Word Wall* Riddles
>
> 1. Number 1 is a word that begins with **al** and fits in this sentence: Why does it _____ rain on football nights? (always)
>
> 2. Number 2 is a word that begins with **al** and fits in this sentence: I didn't finish my home-work but I _____ did. (almost)
>
> 3. Number 3 means the opposite of **dependent**. (independent)
>
> 4. Number 4 means the opposite of **possible**. (impossible)
>
> 5. For number 5, write the seven-letter word that ends with **-able**. (lovable)
>
> 6. For number 6, write the word that rhymes with and is spelled like **bought** and **brought**. (thought)
>
> 7. Number 7 is what is in the middle of a doughnut. (hole)
>
> Answer Key: 1. **always** 2. **almost** 3. **independent** 4. **impossible** 5. **lovable** 6. **thought** 7. **hole**

After students write the words, have them check their own papers by once more chanting the letters aloud, underlining each letter as they say it.

Extending the *Word Wall* to Other Words

Students now have 110 *Word Wall* words they are spelling automatically and fluently. They should also be able to spell lots of other words, including these from previous months:

should	would	cause	cities	communities	country	excite
excited	get	laugh	laughing	school	beauty	cover
covers	covered	covering	recover	recovers	recovered	recovering
discovers	discovered	discovering	rough	tough	hope	hopes
hoped	hoping	hopeful	shouldn't	couldn't	anything	everyone
hiding	troubling	writing	written	special	friend	friendlier
friendliest	newer	newest	real	usual	excitedly	beautifully
hopelessly	hopefully	terribly	generally	unhappy	happy	happily
unhappily	happier	happiest	unhappier	unhappiest	anything	other
confuse	confused	confusing	questioning	questioned	vacationing	vacationed

In addition, students should now be able to spell the following:

depend	dependent	possible	love	excitable	laughable
recyclable	confusable	questionable	bought	brought	ought

The Wheel

Students now have 110 words on the wall. Your job in the time that remains this year is to do enough review and practice with these words so that students can spell them automatically and fluently and can use the common elements to decode and spell other words. In addition to *Be a Mind Reader*, students might enjoy reviewing the words by playing *The Wheel*, a variation on the traditional Hangman game.

For *The Wheel*, draw blanks on the board to represent the letters in a *Word Wall* word. Have students draw the same number of blanks on their papers. Go around the class letting students ask for letters. If the letter is there, write it in the appropriate blank and let the student ask again. Each student can continue asking until they ask for a letter that is not in the word. Then, go on to the next student. The winner is the first person to spell the whole word correctly; he becomes the "teacher" for the next round.

Example Lesson

1. The teacher draws seven blanks on the board and says, "Our first word has seven letters. Al, guess a letter."

2. Al asks for a **t**. There is no **t** so the teacher moves on to Dottie, who asks for an **s**. There is no **s** either. Nor is there an **h**, for which Donna asks. Pat, however, asks for and gets an **a**:

   _ _ _ **a** _ _ _

3. All eyes, including Pat's, are now on the *Word Wall* searching for a seven-letter word without the letters **t**, **s**, or **h**, and with an **a** in the fourth position. The light dawns in Pat's eyes and she quickly asks for **l**, **o**, **v**, **b**, and **e** and wins by correctly spelling **lovable**!

4. Now Pat goes to the board and gets to be the "teacher." She carefully draws nine lines.

5. It is Jim's turn next and he asks for a **c**. Pat fills in a **c** on the first line.

   c _ _ _ _ _ _ _

6. Jim quickly asks for an **o**, which Pat places on the second line.

   c o _ _ _ _ _ _

7. Next, Jim asks for an **s** but there is no **s**. Carlos is next and asks for a **y**, which Pat places on the last blank.

   c o _ _ _ _ _ **y**

8. Carlos asks for **m**, **n**, **u**, **i**, and **t**, and triumphantly spells the word **community**.

9. Carlos now takes the chalk and draws four lines on the board, and the game continues until the time is up.

***The Wheel* is a fast-paced, fun game which focuses student attention on all of the letters and their positions in words.** The only problem is with overexuberant students who realize what the word is and say it aloud when it is not their turn. This tendency can be quickly quashed, however, if you make the rule that if the word is said aloud before the person whose turn it is has a chance, the person whose turn it is automatically wins and becomes the teacher!

What Looks Right?

This month's lesson uses the **oak/oke** patterns. The steps for the lesson are as follows:

1. Write two words on the board which your students can read and spell and which have the patterns.

2. Have students say these words and notice that they rhyme but that they don't have the same spelling pattern.

3. Create two columns on a board or overhead and head them with the words, underlining the spelling patterns. Have the students create these columns on their own papers, writing the words and underlining the spelling patterns.

4. As you say each word, write it both ways. Students should write it the way that looks right to them and then check the word by finding it in the dictionary.

5. Once the correct spelling is verified, erase or cross out the spelling you wrote that is not correct, then continue with the next word.

6. End the lesson by having students review the words with you. Help them to summarize what good spellers do—and don't do. Good spellers don't spell words one letter at a time. They use the spelling patterns they know from other words. If a word does not look right, a good speller tries another pattern for that sound. The dictionary helps the writer check the probable spelling and decide which sound-alike word has the meaning he wants.

Here are the words for this month's lesson. The finished chart should look like this:

<u>oke</u>	<u>oak</u>
~~soke~~	soak
broke	~~broak~~
joke	~~joak~~
~~oke~~	oak
choke	~~choak~~
poke	~~poak~~
smoke	~~smoak~~
spoke	~~spoak~~
~~croke~~	croak
woke	~~woak~~
stroke	~~stroak~~
slowpoke	~~slowpoak~~
provoke	~~provoak~~
artichoke	~~artichoak~~

Word Sorts and Hunts

20 min.

This month's word sorting and hunting activities will review all of the common patterns for the vowel **a.** Here are the steps for this lesson:

❶ Use the reproducible sheets on pages 170-174 to make a transparency for yourself and sorting sheets for the students, or create your own. On the first day, each child has a sort sheet and the teacher has a transparency that looks like this:

<u>Other</u>	<u>a</u>	<u>a</u>	<u>ai</u>	<u>a–e</u>	<u>ay</u>	<u>ar</u>	<u>aw</u>	<u>a</u>	<u>al</u>
have	cat	baby	wait	game	day	car	law	around	legal

❷ Have your students fold their sheets so that they can't see the last four columns—**ar, aw, a,** and **al.** Cover those four columns on your transparency.

❸ Have the children pronounce each of the key words and notice the spelling pattern. Explain that you are going to show words and students must decide in which column each word fits. To go in a column, the word must have the same spelling pattern and the same sound. Help students see that the word **have** has the **a–e** pattern but cannot go in that column because it does not have the same sound as **game.** The "other" column is where they will put the tricky words—the ones that don't follow the logical patterns. To decide where to put each word, students must both look at the letters and listen to the sounds. Challenge them not to let you "trick them" with some of your tricky words!

❹ Show your children 15-20 words which have the vowel **a.** As you show each word, have students pronounce it and write it in the column in which they think it belongs. Choose a child to come write the word in the correct column on your transparency, then continue with the next word. Here are some words for the first day's lesson:

spray	strap	sale	pace	brag	base	bait	drain
lady	waist	waste	paper	crash	ape	crazy	match

❺ On the second day, use the same sheet again, uncover the **ar** and **aw** columns, and keep the last two columns covered. Show another 15-20 words and have students sort them into the first eight columns. Include some words with more than one syllable and help children focus on the syllable that has the **a** in it. Be sure to have students pronounce each word before writing it and remind them to watch for tricky words. They can't just look at the letters but must also listen for the sounds. Here are words for the second day:

thaw	**raw**	**scar**	**replace**	**water**	**chase**
space	**launch**	**seesaw**	**waiter**	**sharpen**	**cashier**
ranches	**vacation**	**capsule**	**purchase**	**hurricane**	**delay**
		acorn			

❻ On the third day, use all columns. Show students another 15-20 words and have them pronounce and then write them in the appropriate columns:

final	**along**	**strawberries**	**royal**	**above**	**awful**
medal	**erase**	**bookmark**	**about**	**birthday**	**Disneyland®**
Superman®	**restrain**	**alone**	**mineral**	**warm**	**bagels**

❼ On the fourth day, do a blind sort. Give the children a new sorting sheet just like the one they used the first three days, and use a new transparency. Pick 15-20 words already sorted but say each word without showing it. Have the children indicate where they think it belongs by putting a finger on the column. When the children are pointing at the column, show them the word and have them write it where it belongs.

❽ The activity for the fifth day is a blind writing sort. Again, choose 15-20 words already sorted on days 1-3 but, instead of showing the word, say each word and have students try to write it in the correct column before you show it.

Depending of the level of your class, you may want to use some of the easier words on this fifth day. If you use more sophisticated words, praise students for writing them in the correct columns even if they are not spelled correctly. Have students correct any incorrect letters after someone writes the word on your transparency. By the end of the fifth day, all of your students should have a much better notion of some of the common spelling patterns for the vowel **a**.

This is how your final chart should look:

<u>Other</u> have	<u>a</u> cat	<u>a</u> baby	<u>ai</u> wait	<u>a–e</u> game	<u>ay</u> day	<u>ar</u> car	<u>aw</u> law	<u>a</u> around	<u>al</u> legal
waste	strap	lady	bait	sale	spray	scar	thaw	along	final
water	brag	crazy	drain	pace	delay	sharpen	raw	above	royal
launch	crash	vacation	waist	base	birthday	bookmark	seesaw	about	medal
purchase	match	acorn	waiter	paper			strawberries	alone	mineral
warm	cashier	bagels	restrain	ape			awful		
	ranches			replace					
	capsule			chase					
	Disneyland®			space					
	Superman®			hurricane					
				erase					

9 Next week, move the children from word sorting to word hunting. Give them another clean sheet with the columns. Tell them that they have one week to find other words that fit the patterns and write them on their sheets. Encourage them to hunt for words everywhere—around the room; on signs; in books they are reading; and while reading in science, social studies, and math. Have them keep their lists secret and encourage them to gather as many words as possible—especially big words—to contribute to the final sort.

10 For the final sort, attach a large piece of butcher paper across the chalkboard. Set up columns just as they were on the original sort sheets, using a different color permanent marker for each. Let children take turns coming to the front of the class and writing one word in its correct column, pronouncing that word, and, for an obscure word, using it in a sentence. Words can be added until the children run out of words or until there is no more room in a particular column. If possible, hang the butcher paper somewhere in the room and encourage your students to continue to look for words for any columns that still have room.

Reading/Writing Rhymes

20 min.

This month, students learn that a very few rhymes can have three spelling patterns. Students should enjoy writing rhymes with **are/air/ear** and **ue/ew/oo**. (Refer to page 52-54 for instructions.)

are	**air**	**ear**
care, dare	air	wear
bare, mare	chair	bear
hare, rare	hair	tear
blare, scare	pair	pear
fare, flare	fair	swear
stare, glare	flair	
spare, spare	stair	
share	Blair	

compare, prepare,   despair, repair, unfair, underwear

*there, their, where

ew	**ue**	**oo**
new, few	true	too
chew, blew	clue	zoo
dew, brew	glue	moo
stew, knew	blue	boo
flew, crew	due	goo
pew, grew	sue	
screw, drew	Sue	
	cue	

cashew, curfew, barbecue, pursue, avenue, subdue,untrue, kangaroo, hullabaloo, shampoo, bamboo, boohoo, peekaboo, buckaroo, tattoo

*do, you, view, to, two, shoe, who

Making Words

20 min.

Here are three *Making Words* lessons for April. (The **/** indicates words that can be made by simply rearranging the same letters.)

Lesson One:	**Secret Word: Chevrolet®**
Letters on strip:	e e o c h l r t v
Make:	hot, cot, clot/colt, love, vote, tree, three/there, lover, voter, other, clever, revolt, Chevrolet®
Sort for: related words:	love, lover vote, voter
rhyming words:	hot, cot, clot tree, three colt, revolt
Transfer Words:	bolt, degree, trot, molt

Lesson Two:	**Secret Word: Oldsmobile®**
Letters on strip:	e i o o b d l l m s
Make:	old, sold, bold, boom, loom, doom, dime, lime, slime/smile/miles, blood, bloom, bloomed, Oldsmobile®
Sort for: related words:	bloom, bloomed
rhyming words:	old, sold, bold boom, loom, doom, bloom dime, lime, slime
Transfer Words:	unfold, chime, broom, prime

Lesson Three:	**Secret Word: Volkswagen®**
Letters on strip:	a e o g k l n s v w
Make:	log, leg, lag, ago, snag, weak/wake, awake, along, alone, snake/sneak, wolves, slogan, Volkswagen®
Sort for: related words:	wake, awake
words beginning with **a**:	ago, awake, along, alone
rhyming words:	lag, snag snake, wake sneak, weak
Transfer Words:	squeak, quake, gag, peak

Using Words You Know

20 min.

Students should now be quite adept at using words they can spell to help them decode and spell lots of other words. **The final step in making them independent decoders is to help them see that all of the words they can spell are available to them as decoding and spelling helps.** To demonstrate this, you might divide them into teams which will accumulate points by using words they know to figure out how to read and spell other words. Here are the steps for this team decoding/spelling challenge:

❶ Seat the team members closely together so that they can quietly consult on each word. Provide them with paper on which to write words they know that will help them.

❷ For the decoding words, show a word to everyone. Give teams one minute to consult and come up with one or more words spelled like, and rhyming with, the word you have shown. At the end of one minute, ask the team whose turn it is to read and spell one known word and decode the shown word. If they are correct, give them two points—one point for having a usable known word and one point for successfully decoding the new word.

❸ Now, go to the other teams and see if they can tell you another word—not the one mentioned by the first team—which would also work. Give them one point for having another usable word. The reason for this step is to show students that there are often lots of words—not just one "magic" word—that can help.

❹ Continue to show students one-syllable words with common patterns. Use fairly uncommon words, but words your students probably would have heard. Here are some possibilities to get you started:

droop	scoop	screen	blast	crank	cream	sling	wreck

❺ Next, use the same procedure to have students decode some longer words in which the last syllables rhyme with words they know. Give teams three points for these words—one for finding a matching rhyming word for the last syllable, one for decoding the last syllable, and one for figuring out the whole word. Just as with one-syllable words, go to other teams for other words that will work and give them one point for each word. Here are some possibilities:

termite	invite	compute	excuse	platform	explore

6 Spelling, of course, is harder because some words have two rhyming patterns and the reader has to know which one looks right. Here are some words, however, which only have one possibility. For these words, say the word, let teams confer to figure out a rhyming word, and have them decide how to spell the word you said. Award points as before, including one point to other teams who come up with other possibilities:

grip	strong	trunk	blush	slink	dwell	smack	brave

7 Finally, here are some three-point words which can't reasonably be spelled any other way:

engrave	suspend	destroy	request	lipstick	submit

Guess the covered **word.**

Guess the covered **word.**

Guess the Covered Word

20 min.

Sometimes, you may want to write a "fascinating facts" paragraph. You might find inspiration for this type of paragraph on a morning TV show, in a newspaper or magazine article, or when browsing the Internet. This paragraph will let your students in on some fascinating facts about koalas.

Koalas

Koalas are native animals in Australia. Koalas are not bears . They are in the same family as kangaroos . Koalas are only the size of jelly beans when they are born. They live for the first six months inside their mothers' pouches. Once they start to wander around, they love to nibble eucalyptus leaves. A very unusual Koala was born recently at the San Diego Zoo . This Koala has a pink nose instead of a black one. Its fur is completely white. The zookeepers named this albino koala Onya-Birri, which means "ghost boy" in the Aborigine language.

Making These Activities Multilevel

Your *Word Wall* now has 110 words, including all of the frequently misspelled words; most common homophones and contractions; and examples for the most common endings, spelling changes, prefixes, and suffixes. All of your students should be spelling all 110 words correctly all of the time. Your accelerated students should be truly remarkable spellers as they use the patterns from *Word Wall* words to spell hundreds of other words.

This month, students learned that occasionally there are three patterns for rhymes, as in your *Reading/ Writing Rhymes* lessons for **are/air/ear** and **ue/ew/oo**. As you go into the final month of school, help all of your students see how they are growing in their decoding and spelling strategies. You may want them to look back at some of their writing from earlier in the year and make a list of words they couldn't spell then but can spell now. Regardless of where they started, both you and they should see that they have moved forward.

Applying Strategies When Reading and Writing

Continue your reminders to students as they begin reading and writing assignments. When you are reading or editing with them, coach them to use strategies as needed by saying things like this:

- Do you know a word that has the **awk** spelling pattern?

- **S-t-r-o-a-k** is a possible way to spell this word, but there is another rhyming pattern. Can you think of other words that rhyme with **stroke** and have a different spelling pattern?

- You spelled **creation** with **s-h-u-n** at the end. It sounds like it should be **s-h-u-n**, but how are big words that sound like that at the end actually spelled?

Remember, to be independent readers and writers, your students must use what they know about words when they need to use it. Word lessons should be multilevel so that everyone can move forward in their understanding about words.

Assess students' progress by looking at writing samples across time, and by observing their reading fluency and use of strategies when they encounter unfamiliar-in-print words. If you keep your eye on this big independent-use goal, they will too.

Month at a Glance

School is almost over. The children look forward to having summer fun. This month, practice, review, and have fun with all of the words and activities students have been learning all year. What a wonderful time to pull out those early writing samples and let students compare them to a current first draft. Let them compare their ability to read and spell new words. Celebrate the growth of all students.

This month, the following will be suggested:

- *Word Wall* words are reviewed and "overlearned" so they will be at the automatic level. Practice should extend to related words. *Wordo* and *What's My Rule?* activities are introduced as practice formats.
- *Using Words You Know* is expanded to a team competition.
- *Guess the Covered Word* is in paragraph form with vacations as the topic.
- *Making Words* lessons focus on vacation words.
- *Reading/Writing Rhymes* explores rhymes with four spelling patterns: **ary/airy/erry/arry** and **ore/oar/oor/our**.
- *Word Sorts and Hunts* explores common patterns for **o**.
- *What Looks Right?* focuses on the **all/awl** patterns.

Here are some time guidelines to consider this month:

Class with Most Children On Grade Level

- 5 minutes *Word Wall* practice daily
- Three 20-minute word lessons each week, including *What Looks Right?, Word Sorts and Hunts, Reading/Writing Rhymes, Using Words You Know, Making Words,* and *Guess the Covered Word*

Class with Most Children Struggling with Grade-Level Material

- 10 minutes *Word Wall* practice daily
- One 20-minute word lesson every day, including *What Looks Right?, Word Sorts and Hunts, Reading/Writing Rhymes, Using Words You Know, Making Words,* and *Guess the Covered Word*

Class with Almost All Children On or Above Grade Level

- 5 minutes *Word Wall* practice daily
- Two 20-minute word lessons each week, picking and choosing from *What Looks Right?, Word Sorts and Hunts, Reading/Writing Rhymes, Using Words You Know, Making Words,* and *Guess the Covered Word*

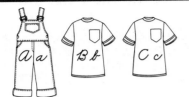

Word Wall

10 min.

As the year comes to a close, students should be much better spellers, not just of these words but lots of other words, as well. The *Word Wall* activities should have focused student attention on the spelling of words, and they should realize that most—but not all—words follow patterns. **A fringe benefit of the *Word Wall* activities should be students' heightened sensitivity to new words they meet.** They should be deciding for themselves whether new words follow the patterns and can be spelled logically or whether there is something illogical in the words.

This month, do as many activities as you can fit in to review, practice, and "overlearn" so that students become so automatic at spelling and using these words that they have them at their fingertips for the rest of their lives.

In addition to the *Word Wall* Words, do activities in which you use the words students can spell based on the *Word Wall* Words:

should	would	cause	cities	communities	country
excite	excited	get	laugh	laughing	school
beauty	cover	covers	covered	covering	recover
recovers	recovered	recovering	discovers	discovered	discovering
rough	tough	hope	hopes	hoped	hoping
hopeful	shouldn't	couldn't	anything	everyone	hiding
troubling	writing	written	special	friend	friendlier
friendliest	newer	newest	real	usual	excitedly
beautifully	hopelessly	hopefully	terribly	generally	unhappy
happy	happily	unhappily	happier	happiest	unhappier
unhappiest	anything	other	confuse	confused	confusing
questioning	questioned	vacationing	vacationed	depend	dependent
possible	love	excitable	laughable	recyclable	confusingly
	questionable	bought	brought	ought	

Present clues such as these in a "riddle" format and have students write the answers:

Word Wall **Riddles**

1. Number 1 is an 11-letter word you can spell if you use parts of **friendly** and **prettiest**, and remember about spelling changes.

2. Number 2 is a contraction that begins with **sh** and is spelled like **wouldn't**.

3. Number 3 is a nine-letter word that you can make from **laugh** and part of **lovable**.

Answer Key: 1. **friendliest** 2. **shouldn't** 3. **laughable**

If students have enjoyed *Be a Mind Reader* (see page 76) and *The Wheel* (see page 129), fit these in when you have a few minutes to sponge up each day. In addition, you might try two other activities, *Wordo*, and *What's My Rule?* Third graders love both of these and the activities focus student attention on the correct spelling of *Word Wall* words.

Wordo

Here is the procedure for *Wordo*:

---

1. To prepare for this bingo-type game, duplicate the *Wordo* sheet on page 175 for each student or make one of your own. Give one sheet to each student.

2. Let several students choose and call out words from the *Word Wall* until you have a total of 24 words. As each word is called, have students chant its spelling and carefully write it in any one of the squares on their sheets. Also, write each word on an index card. Tell students that they must write each word correctly and clearly because if they win (by having all of one row, horizontal, vertical, or diagonal, covered), they must have the words written clearly and spelled correctly. They will all have the same 24 words, but not in the same places. Where they put the words will determine who wins, not whether they have the words.

3. When you have 24 words on index cards and students have 24 words written in the 24 empty boxes, shuffle your cards and begin to call words. Let students cover the words with markers (small, round cereal pieces work well and make a healthy snack when it is time to clean up).

4. When someone completely covers a row, he shouts, "Wordo!" Check his sheet and, if you have called the covered words and he has written them correctly and clearly, he is the winner.

5. Have all students clear their sheets and begin again, letting the winner be the one to call out the words.

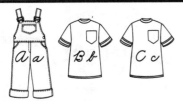 

Most third graders love *Wordo* and, if you emphasize the importance of correct and clear writing of each word, it is great practice. You can use a sheet for several days and then have students make another one with 24 different words. Many teachers do this activity during snack time each day. Some parents may be willing to donate some healthy cereals and tiny crackers to use as markers.

What's My Rule?

What's My Rule? is a sorting game. Here are the directions for one example game:

> 1. To prepare for this game, write some or all of the 110 *Word Wall* words on cards and display them in a pocket chart so that students can manipulate them.
>
> 2. To demonstrate for students how the game works, think of a rule that determines which words you will take and which words you leave. Remove the words that follow your rule and lay them along the chalk ledge. Then, let students guess what your rule was. Imagine, for example, that these were the words you took out of the pocket chart:
>
>   **something   sometimes   myself   anyone   everybody   everything   into**
>
>   Your rule would have been "take only compound words."
>
> 3. When someone guesses the rule, take some other words with another rule in mind:
>
>   **beautiful   because   by   buy   before**
>
>   Students should guess that these words all began with **b**.
>
> 4. Next, take **whole** and **could**. It may take a while for your students to figure out that these are the only words with five letters that contain **o**!

Use *What's My Rule?* to review all of the features of the words you have been studying. You can take words with a spelling change, only those with consonants doubled, contractions, contractions with **c** in them, contractions with four letters, etc. The possibilities are endless. Once students catch on to how *What's My Rule?* is played, let them take over the job of thinking of a rule and picking words. This goes faster if you first have everyone write down the words they will pick and allow you to check the list to make sure it works.

Looks **Right**

Looks **Right**

What Looks Right?

20 min.

This month's lesson uses the **all/awl** patterns. Here are the steps for the lesson:

1. Write two words on the board which your students can read and spell and which have the patterns.

2. Have students say these words and notice that they rhyme but that they don't have the same spelling pattern.

3. Create two columns on a chart or overhead and head them with the words, underlining the spelling patterns. Have the students create these columns on their own papers, writing the words and underlining the spelling patterns.

4. As you say each word, write it both ways. Students should write it the way that looks right to them and then check the word by finding it in the dictionary.

5. Once the correct spelling is verified, erase or cross out the spelling you wrote that is not correct. Continue with the next word.

6. End the lesson by having students review the words with you. Help them summarize what good spellers do—and don't do. Good spellers don't spell words one letter at a time. They use the spelling patterns they know from other words. If a word does not look right, a good speller will try another pattern for that sound. The dictionary will help him check his probable spelling and let him know which sound-alike word has the meaning he wants.

Here are the words for this month's lesson. Your finished chart should look like this:

<u>**all**</u>	<u>**awl**</u>
call	~~cawl~~
hall	~~hawl~~
fall	~~fawl~~
tall	~~tawl~~
small	~~smawl~~
wall	~~wawl~~
mall	~~mawl~~
ball	bawl
~~brall~~	brawl
~~drall~~	drawl
~~scrall~~	scrawl
baseball	~~basebawl~~
snowfall	~~snowfawl~~

Word Sorts and Hunts

This month's word sorting and hunting activities will review some of the common patterns for the vowel **o.** Here are the steps for this lesson:

❶ Use the reproducible sheets on pages 170-174 to make a transparency for yourself and sorting sheets for the students, or create your own. On the first day, each child has a sort sheet and the teacher has a transparency that looks like this:

Other	o	o	oa	o–e	or	oy	ou	ow	ow
work	hot	go	boat	home	for	boy	out	show	now

❷ Have your students fold their sheets so that they can't see the last four columns—**oy, ou, ow,** and **ow.** Cover those four columns on your transparency.

❸ Have the children pronounce each of the key words and notice the spelling pattern. Explain that you will show them words and they must decide in which column each word fits. To go in a column, the word must have the same spelling and the same sound. Help students see that the word **work** has the **"or"** pattern but cannot go in that column because it does not have the same sound as **for**. The "other" column is where they will put the tricky words—the ones that don't follow the logical patterns. To decide where to put each word, they must both look at the letters and listen to the sounds. Challenge them not to let you "trick them" with some of your tricky words!

❹ Show children 15-20 words which have the vowel **o.** As you show each word, have students pronounce the word and then write it in the column in which they think it belongs. Choose a child to write the word in the correct column on your transparency. Then, continue with the next word. Here are some words for the first day's lesson:

old	corn	hope	bone	fog	stock	choke	fort	pro
worm	roll	moan	joke	who	drop	fork	toast	throat

5 On the second day, use the same sheet again, uncover the **oy** and **ou** columns, and keep the last two columns covered. Show another 15-20 words and have students sort them into the first eight columns. Include some words with more than one syllable and help children focus on the syllable that has the **o** in it. Be sure to have students pronounce each word before writing it and remind them to watch for tricky words. They can't just look at the letters but must also listen for the sounds. Here are some words for the second day's lesson:

cloud	toy	hound	enjoy	over	chose	could	tough
oyster	storm	love	expose	perform	pony	telephone	discount
			robber				

6 On the third day, use all columns. Show students another 15-20 words and have them pronounce and then write each in the appropriate column. Suggested words:

clown	glow	thorns	crow	crown	acorn	most	thought
quote	rotten	campground	elbow	flowers	throw	buffalo	coach
			locker	flagpole			

7 On the fourth day, do a blind sort. Give the children a new sorting sheet just like the one they used the first three days, and use a new transparency. Pick 15-20 words already sorted but say each word without showing it. Have the children indicate where they think it belongs by putting a finger on the column. When the children are pointing at the column, show them the word and have them write it where it belongs.

8 The final activity for the fifth day is a blind writing sort. Again, choose 15-20 words already sorted on days 1-3 but, instead of showing each word, say the word and have students try to write it in the correct column before you show it.

Depending of the level of your class, you may want to use some of the easier words on this fifth day. If you use more sophisticated words, praise students for writing them in the correct columns even if the words are not spelled correctly. Have them correct any incorrect letters after someone writes the word on your transparency. By the end of the fifth day, all of your students should have a much better notion of some of the common spelling patterns for the vowel **o**.

The final chart might look like this:

Other **work**	**o** **hot**	**o** **go**	**oa** **boat**	**o–e** **home**	**or** **for**	**oy** **boy**	**ou** **out**	**ow** **show**	**ow** **now**
worm	fog	old	moan	hope	corn	toy	cloud	glow	clown
who	stock	pro	toast	bone	fort	enjoy	hound	crow	crown
could	drop	roll	throat	choke	fork	oyster	discount	elbow	flowers
tough	robber	over	coach	joke	storm		campground	throw	
love	rotten	pony		chose	perform				
thought	locker	most		expose	thorns				
		buffalo		telephone	acorn				
				quote					
				flagpole					

❾ Next week, move the children from word sorting to word hunting. Give them another clean sheet with the same columns. Tell them that they have one week to find other words that fit the patterns and write them on their sheets. Encourage them to hunt for words everywhere—around the room; on signs; in books they are reading; and while reading in science, social studies, and math. Have them keep their lists secret and encourage them to gather as many words as possible—especially big words—to contribute to the final sort.

❿ For the final sort, attach a large piece of butcher paper across the chalkboard. Set up columns just as they were on the original sort sheets, using a different color permanent marker for each. Let children take turns coming to the front of the class and writing one word in its correct column, pronouncing that word, and, for an obscure word, using it in a sentence. Words can be added until the children run out of words or until there is no more room in a particular column. If possible, hang the butcher paper somewhere in the room and encourage your students to continue to look for words for any columns that still have room.

Reading/Writing Rhymes

20 min.

For the final *Reading/Writing Rhymes* lesson, use some rhymes that have four common patterns. In most dialects, **ary**, **airy**, **erry**, and **arry** rhyme. If one of these is pronounced differently where you live, omit that one. The same advice applies to **ore**, **oar**, **oor**, and some words spelled with **our**. Here are the steps for a *Reading/Writing Rhymes* lesson (see pages 52-54 for preparation steps):

Here are some words for this month's charts:

__ary__	__airy__	__erry__	__arry__
Mary, scary	airy	cherry, ferry	carry, marry
Gary, Cary	dairy	Terry, merry	tarry, Harry
vary, wary	hairy	berry	Larry, Barry
	fairy		

canary, January, February, dictionary, military, necessary, ordinary, secretary, raspberry, strawberry

*bury, very

__ore__	__oar__	__oor__	__our__
more, store	roar	door	your
pore, bore	boar	floor	four
sore, snore	soar	poor	pour
chore, gore	uproar		
core, tore			
shore, score			
swore			

ignore, explore, before, seashore

*or, for, war, dinosaur

Month-by-Month Phonics for Third Grade

© Carson-Dellosa CD-2404

20 min.

Making Words

The final three *Making Words* lessons all end in secret words which would be fun places during the summer.

Lesson One:		**Secret Word: seashore**
Letters on strip:		a e e o h r s s
Make:		as, ash, ear, hear, here, hero, nose, rose/sore, shore, shoes, horse, ashes, heroes, seashore
Sort for:	related words:	ash, ashes hero, heroes shore, seashore
	homophones:	here, hear
	rhyming words: (same pattern)	ear, hear nose, rose sore, shore
Transfer Words:		unclear, dispose, score, spear

Lesson Two:		**Secret Word: playground**
Letters on strip:		a o u d g l n p r y
Make:		go, ago, land, long, loud, aloud, proud, along, grand, group, young, angry, pardon, proudly, playground
Sort for:	related words:	proud, proudly loud, aloud
	words beginning with **a**:	ago, along, aloud
	rhyming words:	and, grand loud, proud
Transfer Words:		expand, demand, cloud, brand

Lesson Three:		**Secret Word: campground**
Letters on strip:		a o u c d g m n p r
Make:		dog, dug, drug, drag, camp, moan, groan, cramp, mound, pound, round, ground, dragon, gumdrop, campground
Sort for:	related words:	camp, campground
	rhyming words:	dug, drug camp, cramp moan, groan pound, round, ground, mound, campground
Transfer Words:		sound, shrug, stamp, loan

Using Words You Know

20 min.

Again this month you might divide your class into teams and let them use all of the words they know to decode and spell some new words. Here are the steps for this team decoding/spelling challenge:

❶ Seat the team members close together so that they can quietly consult on each word. Provide them with paper on which to write words they know that will help them.

❷ For the decoding words, show a word to everyone. Give teams one minute to consult and come up with one or more words which are spelled like and rhyme with the word you have shown. At the end of one minute, ask the team whose turn it is to read and spell one known word and decode the shown word. If they are correct, give them two points—one point for having a usable known word and one point for successfully decoding the shown word.

❸ Now, go to the other teams and see if they can tell you another word (not the one mentioned by the first team) which would also work. Give them one point for having another usable word. This step shows students that there are often lots of words—not just one "magic" word—that will help with decoding.

❹ Continue to show teams one-syllable words which have several rhyming words students know. Make your words fairly uncommon words, but words your students probably would have heard. Here are some possibilities to get you started:

trace	shade	shrink	scope	swore	cross	stock	drown

❺ Next, use the same procedure to have teams decode some two-syllable words in which the last syllable rhymes with words students know. Give teams three points for these words—one for finding a matching rhyming word for the last syllable, one for decoding the last syllable, and one for figuring out the whole word. Just as with one-syllable words, go to other teams for other words that will work and give one point for a usable word. Here are some possibilities:

toothpick	landscape	revoke	campsite	repeat	provoke

❻ Spelling, of course, is harder because some words have two rhyming patterns and the writer must know which one looks right. Below are some words, however, which only have one possibility. For these words, say the word and let teams confer to figure it out. Award points as before, including one point to other teams which come up with other possibilities.

split	scold	slump	pry	prick	chest	blend	crank

❼ Here are some three-point words for teams to spell that can't reasonably be spelled any other way:

convoy	program	expand	display	contrast	defend

Guess the covered word.

Guess the covered word.

Guess the Covered Word

20 min.

Finally, summer is here and many students would love to spend the summer traveling to faraway places. Why not write a "fantasy" paragraph telling where some of your adventurous kids might go "if they could have their wish"?

Summer Travel

What if we were all granted one wish and could go anywhere in the world this summer? Karen might go to Switzerland and climb the tallest mountain. Dottie might spend the summer at the coast in Rhode Island. Brad and Rom might go to Disneyland®. Cassie might fly to London. Marty might spend the summer fishing at Lake Norman. David might go on a safari in Africa. Mrs. C. might go to Hawaii and take everyone in the class with her!

Making These Activities Multilevel

As this year comes to a close, we hope that you have enjoyed doing all of the different word activities with your class. We hope that there has been enough variety so that all of your students have moved forward in their decoding and spelling. Most of all, we hope that you have seen real differences in students' use of word strategies as they actually read and write.

Do you have a better concept now of how to make an activity multilevel? Meeting the range of children in any class is the biggest challenge most third-grade teachers face. We hope this book has helped you to do this. Remember that next year's class will be different. You will once again have to decide what kind of adaptations to make so that the word activities you do can stretch to meet the greatest range of children.

Applying Strategies When Reading and Writing

By now, your students should be much better decoders and spellers. **Help them to "verbalize" what they do so that they will continue to use these strategies when you are no longer there to remind them.** Ask them questions such as these:

Question 1

"Why did we put these words on the wall, practice them, and try to make sure that we always spelled them correctly in any writing?"

Students should be able to verbalize that some words aren't spelled logically. The brain makes things automatic after doing them a certain number of times; this is helpful if you are doing them right and disastrous if you are doing them wrong. To get wrong things out of the automatic compartment and replace them with correct things, you have to have as much practice as you did getting the wrong things in there in the first place.

Help students realize that there may be other words they have wrong in their automatic spelling compartments. When they notice these words, they need to develop some independent strategies for rooting them out and replacing them. One of the authors of this book does this by placing tiny self-stick notes along the top of the computer with words such as **no one** (which ought to be a compound word like **someone**, **anyone**, and **everyone**) and **receive** (it is distracting to have to repeat the mnemonic rhyme every time you need to spell it). Eventually, when the correct spelling of these words is firmly placed in the automatic compartment, these self-stick notes are removed and thrown away.

Question 2

"Why have we been using words we know to help us with spelling and decoding other words?"

Help students verbalize that "that's how your brain works." When it sees something new, it goes looking for other things which are similar to help make sense of the new thing. We call these similar things patterns. In short words, the major patterns are rhyming words. Thinking of a word that is spelled the same, and making the new word rhyme with that word, is a quick and efficient decoding strategy. This helps with spelling too, except that in English, there are sometimes two patterns for the same rhyme. The brain develops a visual checking system by putting familiar words with other words having the same pattern.

Question 3

"What can you do when you write a word and notice that it doesn't look right, or you are sure you haven't spelled it correctly?"

If you write a word and it doesn't look right, you should try writing it with another rhyming pattern. If it is really important, you can check your spelling—or see which sound-alike word has the right meaning—by looking it up in the dictionary.

In English, lots of words are related through their root words, prefixes, and suffixes. Have students identify the *Word Wall* words that help them decode and spell lots of other words. Being able to spell these words so well and fast means they are readily available at the fronts of the word stores in our brains to help us decode and spell hundreds of other words.

Question 4

"What good will it do to know these things about words if you don't use them while reading and writing?"

None! We decode and spell words so that we can read and write!

Portable Word Wall—August/September

A	B	C	D	E	F	G	H
again	because	could			favorite		have

I	J	K	L	M	N	O	P
into						off	people

Q	R	S	T	U	V	W	XYZ
		said	they	until	very	want who	

154

Month-by-Month Phonics for Third Grade

Portable Word Wall—October

A
again

B
because

C
could
city
community
countries

D

E
exciting

F
favorite

G
getting

H
have

I
into

J

K

L
laughed

M

N

O
off

P
people
pretty
prettier
prettiest

Q

R

S
said
schools

T
they
to
too (also)
two (#2)

U
until

V
very

W
want
who
was

XYZ

Portable Word Wall—November

A
again

B
because
beautiful
before

C
could
city
community
countries

D
discover

E
exciting
enough

F
favorite
first

G
getting

H
have
hopeless

I
into

J
journal

K

L
laughed
let's

M

N

O
off

P
people
pretty
prettier
prettiest

Q

R
recycle

S
said
schools

T
they
to
too (also)
two (#2)
their
there
they're (they are)

U
until

V
very

W
want
who
was
went
when

XYZ

© Carson-Dellosa CD-2404

Month-by-Month Phonics for Third Grade

Portable Word Wall—December

𝒜
again
anyone
are

ℬ
because
beautiful
before

C
could
city
community
countries
can't

𝒟
discover
don't

ℰ
exciting
enough
everybody
everything

ℱ
favorite
first

𝒢
getting

ℋ
have
hopeless
hidden

ℐ
into

𝒥
journal

𝒦

ℒ
laughed
let's

ℳ

𝒩

𝒪
off
our

𝒫
people
pretty
prettier
prettiest

𝒬

ℛ
recycle
right

𝒮
said
schools

𝒯
they
to
too (also)
two (#2)
their
there
they're (they are)
terrible
trouble

𝒰
until

𝒱
very

𝒲
want
who
was
went
when
won't
wouldn't
write (pencil)

𝒳𝒴𝒵

Portable Word Wall—January

A
again
anyone
are
about

B
because
beautiful
before

C
could
city
community
countries
can't

D
discover
don't

E
exciting
enough
everybody
everything
especially
except

F
favorite
first
friendly

G
getting

H
have
hopeless
hidden

I
into

J
journal

K
knew
know

L
laughed
let's

M
myself

N
new (old)
no (yes)

O
off
our

P
people
pretty
prettier
prettiest
probably

Q

R
recycle
right
really

S
said
schools

T
they
to
too (also)
two (#2)
their
<u>there</u>
they're (they are)
terrible
trouble

T
then

U
until
usually

V
very

W
want
who
was
went
when
won't
wouldn't
write (pencil)
what

XYZ

Month-by-Month Phonics for Third Grade

Portable Word Wall—February

A
- again
- anyone
- are
- about

B
- because
- beautiful
- before
- by
- buy (sell)

C
- could
- city
- community
- countries
- can't

D
- discover
- don't
- didn't
- doesn't

E
- exciting
- enough
- everybody
- everything
- especially
- except

F
- favorite
- first
- friendly

G
- getting
- general
- governor

H
- have
- hopeless
- hidden

I
- into

J
- journal

K
- knew
- know

L
- laughed
- let's

M
- myself

N
- new (old)
- no (yes)

O
- off
- our
- one (#1)

P
- people
- pretty
- prettier
- prettiest
- probably

Q

R
- recycle
- right
- really

S
- said
- schools
- something
- sometimes

T
- then
- they
- to
- too (also)
- two (#2)
- their
- there
- they're (they are)
- terrible
- trouble

U
- until
- usually
- unhappiness

V
- very

W
- want
- who
- was
- went
- when
- won't
- wouldn't
- write (pencil)
- what

X Y Z
- winner
- won
- your
- you're (you are)

Portable Word Wall—March

A
again
anyone
are
about
another

B
because
beautiful
before
by
buy (sell)

C
could
city
community
countries
can't
confusion

D
discover
don't
didn't
doesn't

E
exciting
enough
everybody
everything
especially
except

F
favorite
first
friendly

G
getting
general
governor

H
have
hopeless
hidden

I
into
I'm
its
it's (it is)

J
journal

K
knew
know

L
laughed
let's

M
myself

N
new (old)
no (yes)

O
off
our
one (#1)

P
people
pretty
prettier
prettiest
probably

Q
question

R
recycle
right
really

S
said
schools
something
sometimes

T
then
that's
threw (ball)
through

TH
they
to
too (also)
two (#2)
their
there
they're (they are)
terrible
trouble

U
until
usually
unhappiness

V
very
vacation

W
want
who
was
went
when
won't
wouldn't
write (pencil)
what
winner
won
we're (we are)
wear (cap)
where
with

XYZ
your
you're (you are)

Portable Word Wall—April

a
again
anyone
are
about
another
almost
also
always

B
because
beautiful
before
by
buy (sell)

C
could
city
community
countries
can't
confusion

D
discover
don't
didn't
doesn't

E
exciting
enough
everybody
everything
especially
except

F
favorite
first
friendly

G
getting
general
governor

H
have
hopeless
hidden
hole (doughnut)

I
into
I'm
its
it's (it is)
impossible
independent

J
journal

K
knew
know

L
laughed
let's
lovable

M
myself

N
new (old)
no (yes)

O
off
our
one (#1)

P
people
pretty
prettier
prettiest
probably

Q
question

R
recycle
right
really

S
said
schools
something
sometimes

T
then
that's
threw (ball)
through
thought
they
to
too (also)
two (#2)
their
there
they're (they are)
terrible
trouble

U
until
usually
unhappiness

V
very
vacation

W
want
who
was
went
when
won't
wouldn't
write (pencil)
what
winner
won
we're (we are)
wear (cap)
where
with
were
weather (cloud)
whether
whole

XYZ
your
you're (you are)

Month-by-Month Phonics for Third Grade

Making Words Strips—October

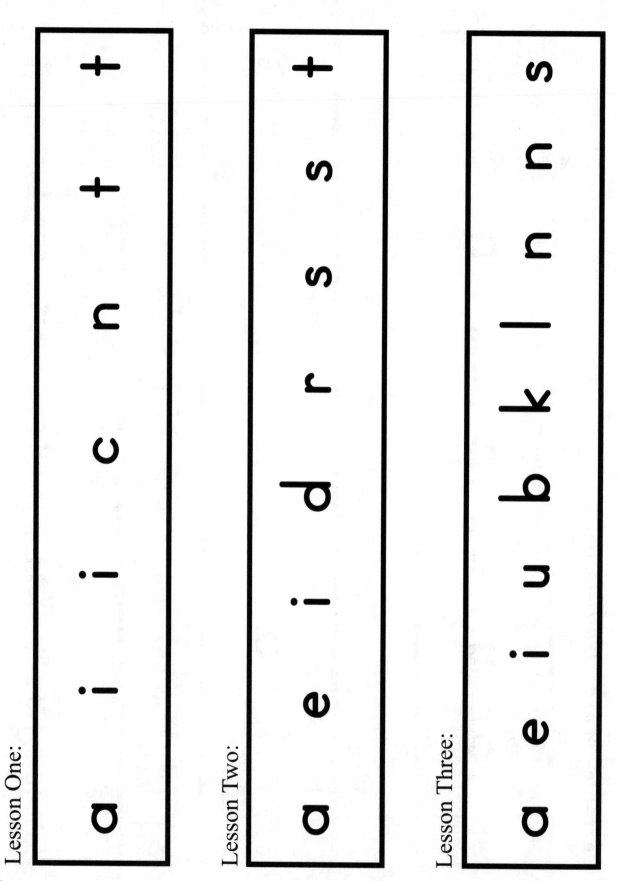

Lesson One:

a i i c n t t

Lesson Two:

a e i d r s s

Lesson Three:

a e i u b k l n n s

Month-by-Month Phonics for Third Grade

Making Words Strips—November

Lesson One: i o u c m m n t y

Lesson Two: e i o b g h n r s

Lesson Three: i o h r s t y

Making Words Strips—December

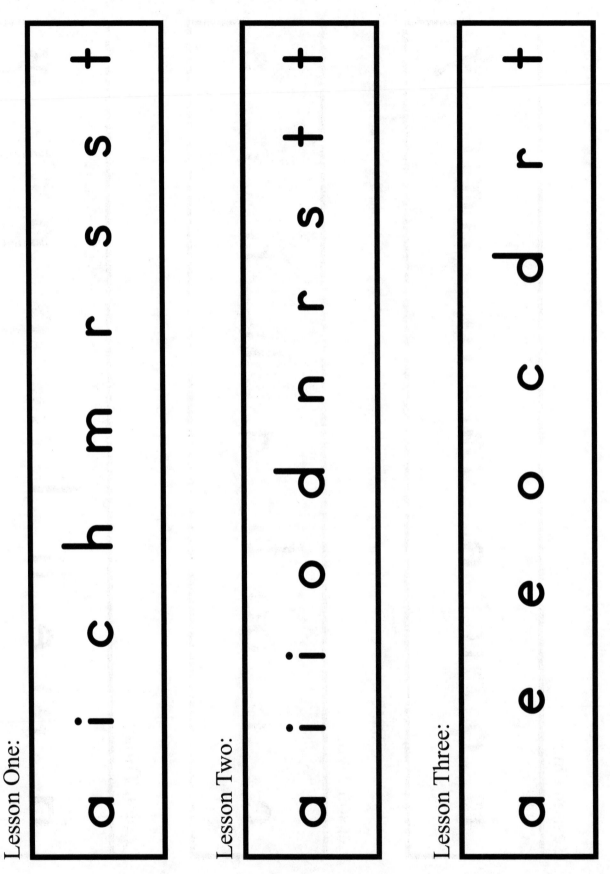

Lesson One: a i c h m r s s t

Lesson Two: a i i o d n r s t t

Lesson Three: a e e o c d r t

Month-by-Month Phonics for Third Grade

Making Words Strips—January

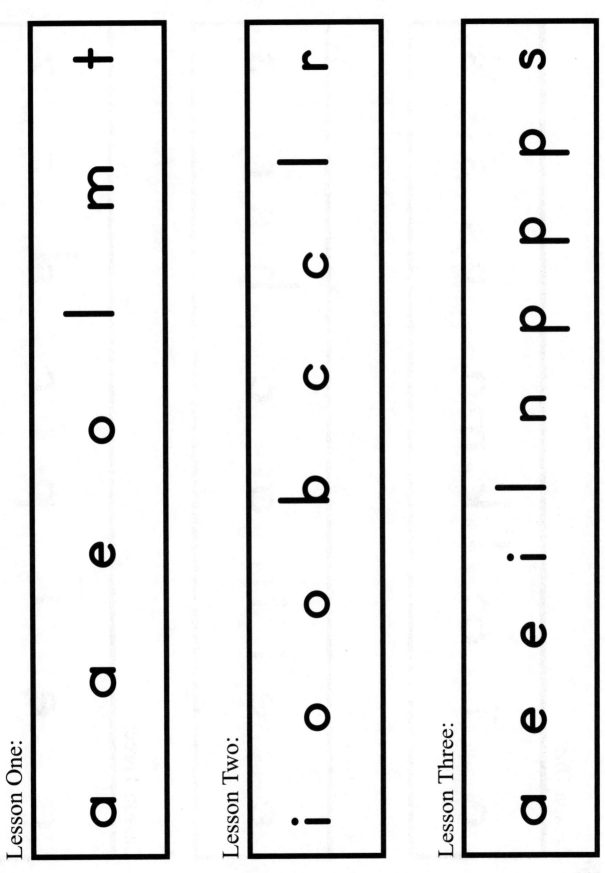

Lesson One:

a a e o l m t

Lesson Two:

i o o b c c l r

Lesson Three:

a e e i l n p p p s

Making Words Strips—February

Lesson One:

s r n k c i e

Lesson Two:

s r h c o i e e

Lesson Three:

z t s r p l e e

Lesson One:

e e i i c c l r t t y

Lesson Two:

a e e i b r s t t

Lesson Three:

a e i c g m n t

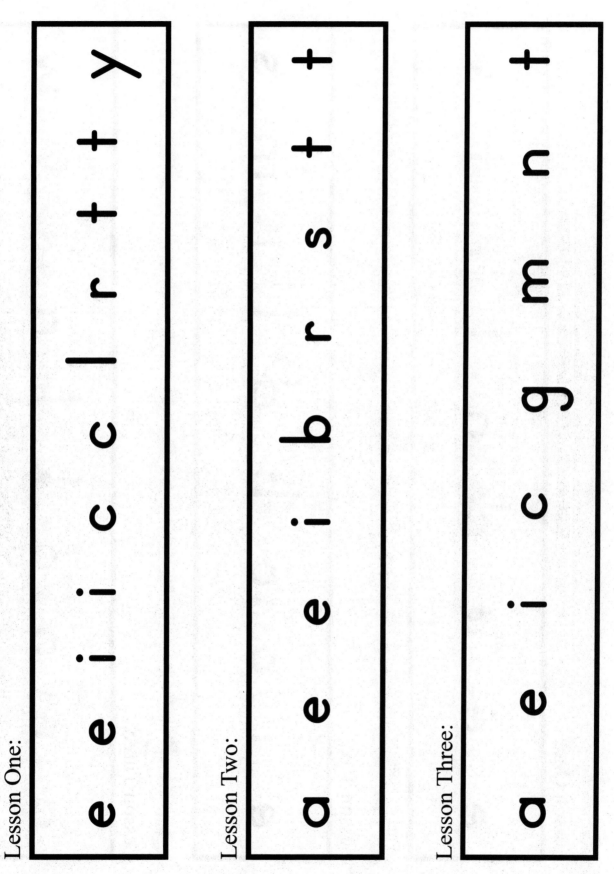

Making Words Strips—April

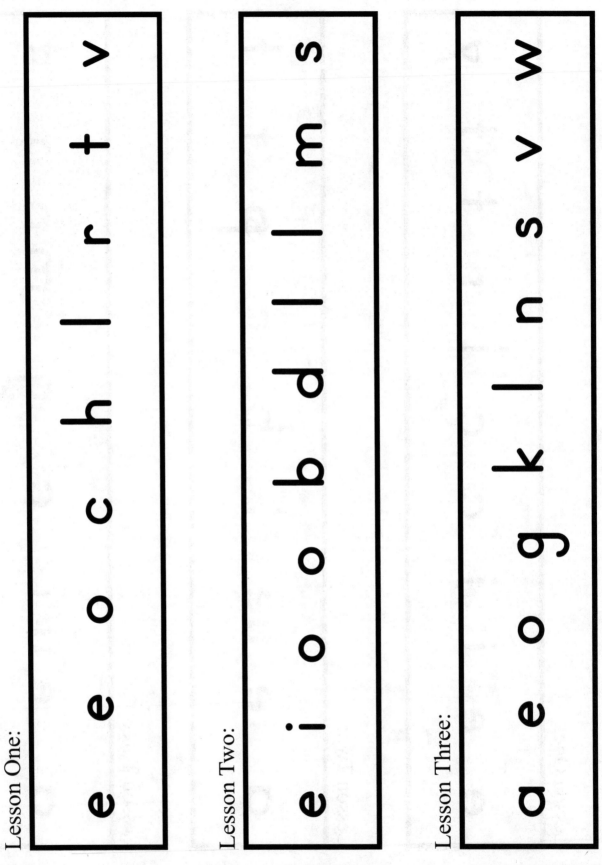

Lesson One: e   e   o   c   h   l   r   t   v

Lesson Two: e   i   o   o   b   d   l   l   m   s

Lesson Three: a   e   o   g   k   l   n   s   v   w

Month-by-Month Phonics for Third Grade   © Carson-Dellosa CD-2404

Making Words Strips—May/June

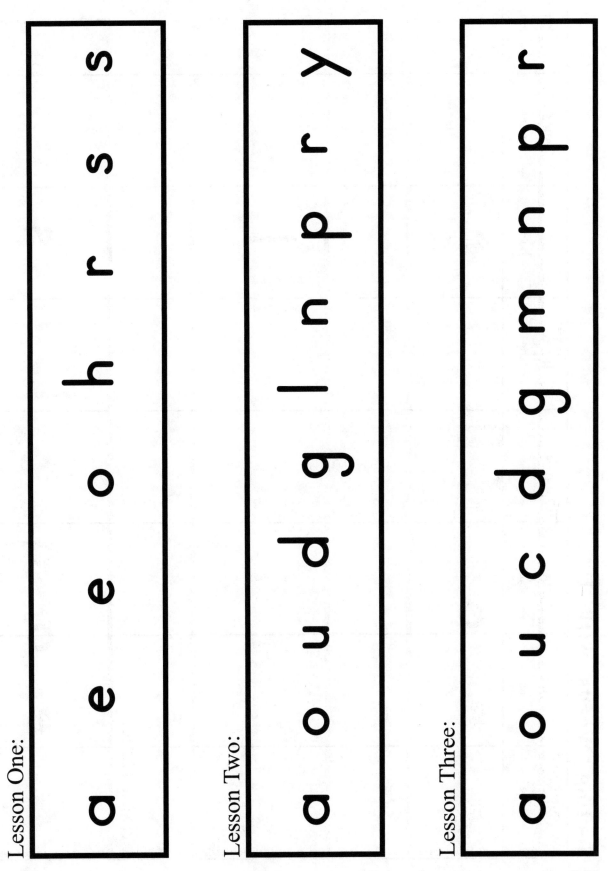

Lesson One: a e e o h r s s

Lesson Two: a o u d g l n p r y

Lesson Three: a o u c d g m n p r

Sorting Words with U

Other judge	u us	ue blue	u–e use	u–e tune	ur burn	sure insure	ture nature

Month-by-Month Phonics for Third Grade

Sorting Words with I and Y

Other give	i it	ie die	i–e nice	ir bird	y my	y happy	tion nation	sion mansion

Sorting Words with E

Other earth	e he	e pet	ee tree	ea eat	ea bread	er her	ew new	le little

Month-by-Month Phonics for Third Grade

Sorting Words with A

Other have	a cat	a baby	ai wait	a-e game	ay day	ar car	aw law	a around	al legal

Sorting Words with O

Other work	o hot	o go	oa boat	o–e home	or for	oy boy	ou out	ow show	ow now

Month-by-Month Phonics for Third Grade

WORDO

W	O	R	D	O
		FREE		

REFERENCES

Caine, R. N. and Caine, G. (1991) *Teaching and the Human Brain*. Association for Supervision and Curriculum Development.

Cunningham, P. M. and Hall, D. P. (2001) *Making Words Lessons for Home or School (Grade 3)*. Greensboro, NC: Carson-Dellosa Publishing.

Cunningham, P. M., Hall, D. P., and Cunningham, J. W. (2000) *Guided Reading the Four-Blocks® Way*. Greensboro, NC: Carson-Dellosa Publishing.

Cunningham, P. M., Hall, D. P., Kohfeldt, J. (1998) *Word Wall "Plus" for Third Grade*. Greensboro, NC: Carson-Dellosa Publishing.

Cunningham, P. M., Hall, D. P., and Gambrell, L. G. (2002) *Self-Selected Reading the Four-Blocks® Way*. Greensboro, NC: Carson-Dellosa Publishing.

Cunningham, P. M., Hall, D. P., and Sigmon, C. M. (1999) *The Teachers' Guide to the Four Blocks®*. Greensboro, NC: Carson-Dellosa Publishing.

Cunningham, P. M. and Allington, R. L. (2003) *Classrooms that Work: They Can All Read and Write*, 3rd ed. Boston, MA: Allyn & Bacon.

Hall, D. P. and Cunningham, P. M. (2003) *The Administrators' Guide to the Four Blocks*. Greensboro, NC: Carson-Dellosa Publishing.

Henderson, E. H. (1990) *Teaching Spelling* (2nd ed.). Boston, MA: Houghton Mifflin Co.

Young, S. (1994) *Scholastic Rhyming Dictionary*. New York, NY: Scholastic.